> *"Change yourself and change the world."*
>
> Anonymous

Your Rebel Dreams

Rebel Diva Book One

Find Your Calling

A fantastic journey to uncover your purpose and passions in life.

Copyright © 2019 Tikiri Herath
Edition: 2019
Library & Archives Canada Cataloging in Publication
ISBN: 978-1-989232-00-2

Author: Tikiri Herath
Publisher: The Rebel Diva Academy®
Proofread and Editing: Stephanie Parent
Copy Editing: Deborah Dove
Cover Design: Angela O e-covers
Formatting: Aelurus Publishing
Author Shot: Aura Mckay

All rights reserved. The use of any part of this publication, reproduced, transmitted in any form or by any means electronic, mechanical, photocopying, recording, or otherwise or stored in a retrieval system without prior written consent of the publisher—or in the case of photocopying or other reprographic copying, a license from the Canadian Copyright Licensing Agency—is an infringement of the copyright law.

Tikiri

The advice and strategies contained here may not be suitable or applicable to everyone or to every situation. Reading this work does not construe an engagement between the author/publisher and the reader, and the author/publisher is not rendering any legal, psychological, accounting or any other professional services through this work. Neither the author nor the publisher will be liable for damages arising from here.

The books and website links cited here are only for information and educational purposes and does not mean the author or the publisher endorses everything provided via these external resources. While the author will make every effort to ensure the links in this book remain updated, there is no guarantee the external sites may always be available or provide what they had initially.

TABLE OF CONTENTS

Rebel Defined	vii
An Exclusive Gift	ix
The Fire in Your Belly	11
Who This Book Is For	15
The Heroine's Journey	19
The Passion Pyramid	23
INTRODUCTION	29
SECTION One: My Values	67
SECTION Two: My Flair	105
SECTION Three: My Zone	123
SECTION Four: My Joy	153
SECTION Five: My Service	173
SECTION Six: My Vision	203
SECTION Seven: My Pledge	231
Bonus Section	237
Exclusive Gift	244
About the Author	250
A Free Story	251

Own Your Life. Be a Rebel Diva.

Rebel

NOUN

plural: rebels

Pronunciation /ˈrɛb(ə)l/

A person who resists authority, control, or convention.

Diva

NOUN

plural: divas

Pronunciation /ˈdēvə/

Goddess. Feminine of divus divine. Late 19th century Italian derived from Latin.

I dedicate this book to *you.*

These books are for you if you long, more than anything, to burst out of your shell into the open and live the life you dream about.

To you I say, never stop dreaming. And never, ever give up the pursuit of your passions.

The Rebel Diva Workbooks

www.RebelDivas.com

Sign up to get your exclusive gift!

This Rebel Diva booklet comes with three essential decision-making tools to help you overcome any anxieties when faced with life's challenges. Click on the cover or go to the link below to get your free copy and also learn about exclusive and free training at the Rebel Diva Academy.

Bust Your Fears

https://www.RebelDivas.com/rebel-dreams-gifts/

Your Rebel Dreams

> *"I wish I were a girl again, half savage and hardy and free... Why am I so changed? I'm sure I should be myself were I once among the heather on those hills."*
>
> *Emily Brontë*

A FIRE IN YOUR BELLY

We all hold a precious dream within us—a fire burning in our belly.

Yes, each and every one of us.

Some of us hide our dreams because we're too scared to look our truth in the face. And some of us have valiantly tried to bring those dreams out in the open, but quickly stashed them away because of what someone said or how someone judged us. Then, there are those who ignore their dreams, pretending they don't exist because acknowledging them would mean they'd be compelled to do something.

The end result is graveyards full of women who've been buried with their dreams untouched. Imagine what they could have achieved if they'd stood proudly and taken ownership of their future. Imagine what inspiration they'd have given to the next generation of girls, creating a ripple effect that uplifts us all.

THE WORLD IS YOURS

We're all capable, *more* than capable, of bringing our dreams to light. Every one of us.

Yes, that means *you*.

This world can be yours. The future can be yours. All you need to do is bravely step up, grab life by the horns and ride it. You must take ownership of your future. No one else can do that for you. And there is no better time to start your life's amazing ride than today.

IGNORE THE NAYSAYERS

Why do we wait for a life-changing event like sickness, death, layoff, bankruptcy, separation, or divorce—times when we don't have a choice but to wake up and make drastic changes? Why let others dictate who we are and what we must do?

Most people go through their days in a trance without understanding who they truly are, what they're doing or where they're going.

We, especially women, feel burdened by the expectations others put on us, or many times, by the demands we place on ourselves. Without a clear vision for our lives, we're easily manipulated to meet the desires of others—people who've already figured out what they want in life.

Naysayers can be persistent and hard to ignore, especially if they're family and friends. But if you can summon the courage to stand in your power, you'll get an enormous boost in your energy, vitality, and happiness. This is what will catapult you to your dream life.

Remember, how others may judge us is only a reflection of their own insecurities, fears, and worries, or their need to keep us under their control.

So, stop listening to what they say, stop settling for mediocrity and start following your dreams right this minute.

SUMMON YOUR COURAGE

First, find an ounce of courage inside you.

Then, do some soul-searching and look for those aspirations longing to jump out. Protect and nurture those dreams. Finally, you must take action. In the end, all the dreaming and wishing and hoping in the world won't make anything come alive. Only pure action will do so.

This doesn't have to be scary or difficult. This can be a fun and fulfilling ride. And you're not alone. We will take this journey together.

These books were designed to take you by the hand on an expedition of self-discovery, goal setting, and habit-forming so you can start living your life—the one you desire, not the one others expect of you.

Don't be afraid to stand at the edge of your comfort zone. Feel that tingle of fear mixed with excitement and give it a whirl with plenty of support and cheering from the rest of us. You'll find your sense of self-worth will grow and your inner strength surge. You'll wake up every day feeling good about yourself and confident in who you are.

More importantly, your vision will expand and you'll see beyond yourself. And this is where magic happens. When you grow, the lives of those surrounding you will also grow. You'll become a positive role model for your daughters, your sisters, your neighbors, your colleagues, and more.

This is what will make you a true Rebel Diva. A strong and proud woman who stands in her own power and inspires those around her. You'll become the wonder woman we all look up to.

Now, isn't that a life worth living?

Your Rebel Dreams

> *"An unexamined life is not worth living."*
> Socrates

MY GOAL

My goal is to shake you out of your complacency. My aim is to spur you to uncover the amazing gifts you have within you. I want you to burst out with confidence and put a dazzling smile on your face that says, Watch out world, here I come!

BUT THESE BOOKS AREN'T FOR EVERYONE

I could have easily created a few pop quizzes and slapped on a sexy title like *"The One-Minute Passion Finder,"* and sold a ton of books. But I'd be lying.

I could have filled pages and pages with pointless platitudes to make you feel good about staying stuck where you are and make a handsome profit. But I'd be cheating.

These books don't give you false shortcuts or magic bullets to solve your problems. I call things as they are and don't mince my words.

So, if you don't want to hear hard truths or ask introspective questions, these workbooks aren't for you. If you dislike addressing issues head-on or if you're not a fan of political incorrectness, I urge you not to read further, as it will only aggravate you and I'd hate to do that to you.

If, however, you're looking for practical tips that give you results and don't mind language that is to the point, then read on.

LASTING CHANGE

Lasting change doesn't happen overnight.
Change requires courage. And courage requires conviction.

These books are for the women of this world who yearn to empower themselves, seek the courage to follow their own paths and live lives true to their callings.

If you are willing to do the work to enhance your inner strength and create a lasting impression in your future, you're in the right place. If you're prepared to go against everything you've been taught and do the things the majority of the world won't dare, these books will open new horizons for you.

In these workbooks, you'll find ways to feed the fire burning in your belly. You'll get in touch with your passions. And you'll feel the fear but do it anyway, without worrying about what others think or say.

And that, my dear sisters, is what makes you a true Rebel Diva.

"If an egg is broken by an outside force, life ends. If it's broken by an inside force, life begins. Great things always begin from inside."

Jim Kwik

Your Rebel Dreams

> *"I am a woman with thoughts and questions and shit to say.
> I say if I'm beautiful. I say if I'm strong.
> You will not determine my story – I will."*
>
> *Amy Schumer*

THE HEROINE IS YOU. THE JOURNEY IS YOUR LIFE.

THE HEROINE'S JOURNEY

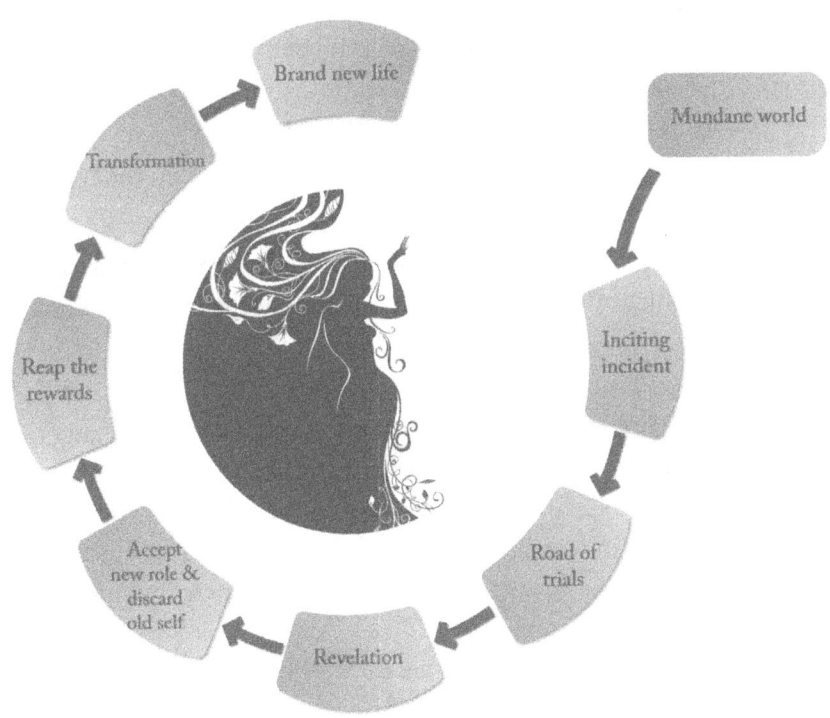

The heroine's journey* is universal.

It applies to you whether you live in the southern hemisphere or the northern one. It pertains to you regardless of your culture, religion, age, race, sexual orientation or anything else that makes you human.

We all start at stage one—the everyday world—until an incident too arduous for us to handle falls on us, forcing us through this cycle. If we're not ready, the road ahead can be a treacherous one with many troubles along the way.

Some of us may never recover from the inciting incident and succumb to it. Others may get lost along the way, taking wrong turns and feeling every strain of their journey. Then, there will be some of us who will carry on pretending to live in the same ordinary world, though everything has changed. We'll be living an illusion which will cause us to crash and burn even more than the original event.

Whether you like it or not, we all undergo this cycle in our lives. And for some of us, more than once. It's inevitable. It's what being human is all about.

So, what do we do?

There are two questions you can ask yourself:

> ✿ Am I going to sit and wait for life-changing events to trip me up, or can I proactively create the life I deserve starting today?

> ✿ Am I going to think of negative incidents as hopeless failures, or can I look at them as calls to adventure—calls to create a brand-new life?

We're all going to come across times when we feel sorrow, anger, or fear. These emotions may come from something that happened, what someone said, or even a mistake we made that leaves us berating ourselves for days on end. Feeling bad (in its many different forms) is normal. It's when we don't face our emotions, run away from them or blame others that problems arise.

We have to learn to acknowledge our feelings. We need to look at what happened dead straight in the eye and decide how we will respond to it. We need to take control of how we resolve the difficult things we face in life. All this means pushing our fears and worries away and moving over to the driver's seat to become the navigators of our own futures.

If you want to take the reins to your life and make it an exciting adventure, these workbooks will show you how.

In these pages, you will find the ideas and concepts that put you in the driver's seat. This doesn't mean you'll be immune to all the troubles of life, but you will have the foresight, the tools, and the knowledge to maneuver your way around them with the least pain and the most gain to you.

Are you ready to become the heroine of your own life?

Based on Joseph Campbell's legendary theory of the twelve-step Hero's Journey.

Your Rebel Dreams

THE PASSION PYRAMID

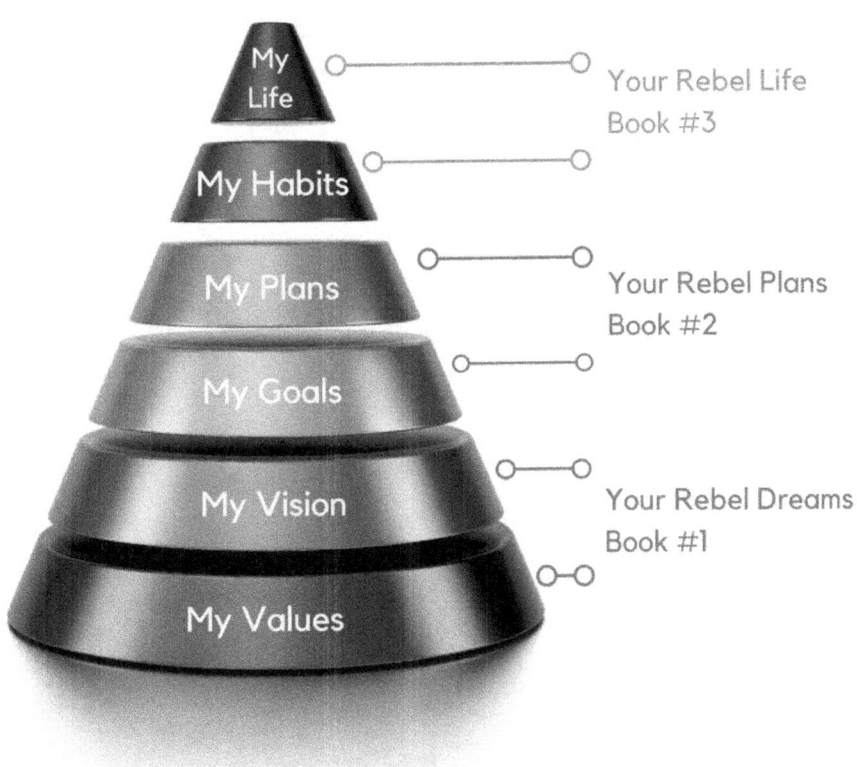

Your Rebel Dreams

"I am no bird and no net ensnares me. I am a free human being with an independent will."
Jane Eyre

THE PASSION PYRAMID

To take control over your life, you will need to have a clear vision and a road map to get there. You will also need to embrace the right mindset and habits.

The Rebel Diva series has been designed to provide you with that knowledge and skill, with easy-to-follow exercises based on the Passion Pyramid.

As the pyramid shows, your life vision is based on your personal values, your goals are derived from your vision, and your plans will come from your goals. Ultimately, your vision, your goals, and your plans will all be sustained by your daily habits and mindset. This is what will help you achieve your dreams and create the life you desire.

For this to work best, you'll have to:

- Be uncompromising on your personal values
- Be resolute in your life vision
- Be intentional, yet savvy, with your goals
- Be focused but adaptable with your plans
- Be regular and consistent in your habits

THE REBEL DIVA BOOKS

Each of the Rebel Diva books focuses on a couple steps of this pyramid, moving from the base to the top.

The first book—*Your Rebel Dreams*—helps you uncover your why, that is, your purpose and your passions, culminating in your what, which is your vision.

The second book—*Your Rebel Plans*—shows you how to design a life around your new vision. It captures the stages of goal setting, action planning, and tracking your progress.

The third book—*Your Rebel Life*—helps you create and foster the right habits in the ten most important pillars of your life, so you can pursue your aspirations with joy.

THIS BOOK BELONGS TO

Rebel Diva	

Location	

Date	

PRINT EXERCISES IN BOOK

Download the PDF worksheet booklet for *Your Rebel Dreams*.

This 100+ page booklet includes worksheets for all the exercises in this book. You can print them, write your answers directly on them, pin them up if you'd like and refer to them every day.

Just visit the website address below to download your free private copy.

https://www.RebelDivas.com/rebel-dreams-gifts/

INTRODUCTION

LET'S BEGIN THIS JOURNEY!

"Don't be afraid of your fears. They're not there to scare you. They're there to let you know that something is worth it."
— C. JoyBell C.

ANYTHING IS POSSIBLE

If you're holding this book in your hands, you have more opportunities, liberties, and choices than most people on Earth.

The young women in my international thrillers, the Red-Heeled Rebels series, come from the slums of India, the brothels of Europe, and the villages of Africa to fight for their rights. They may be fictional characters, but their lives are real.

Did you know that half the world—that's almost three billion of our fellow human beings at the time this book was published—lives on less than $2.50 a day? Among them, almost half a billion are women who cannot read or write. Can you even imagine how an impoverished and illiterate woman would live, eat, and sleep and how she will be treated?

Our lives are their heaven.

So why, then, are so many of us drowning in discontent? Why do we, who can read, write, and have our basic needs met, feel so disenfranchised?

Many of us aren't in as awful circumstances as some of our sisters around the world. We have more privileges and rights than we've ever had before, yet we remain shackled by the chains in our own minds. Instead of getting beaten down by human traffickers, child-bride brokers, and misogynistic communities, like the young women in my novels do, we're beaten down by our own ruminations, insecurities, and irrational worries of what others might think of us.

And so, we stick to jobs we hate. We remain in loveless marriages. We maintain relationships that are dispiriting and we let others sap our energy. We stay in environments that harm us more than nurture us. And our unhappiness continues.

Most of us who are reading this book live in free and open societies with the world at our fingertips. We have all the possibilities to take us wherever we wish to go. Yes, even for those of us who feel like we're in the depths of despair, the world is still our oyster, if we only open our eyes to look.

Unlike many women around the world, we have the freedom of education, movement, and expression. We have options. We have choices. Our future is in our hands—more than we think.

We just have to find the courage to open our eyes wide and step out with gumption and grace.

Wait. We can do better than that.

We can be bold.

We can burst out into the open with confidence and courage to show the world who we truly are. *Who we truly are!*

WE LIVE IN THE BEST ERA IN THE HISTORY OF HUMANKIND

The Internet is the greatest democratizing tool on the planet. It's one of the most extraordinary inventions in modern times, with more than half the population on Earth now using it to share, teach, learn, connect and tell stories.

Today, more than ever, there's an infinite number of tutorials, training, coaching sessions, and educational material on every topic under the sun. Most available for free. We can watch and model successful peers, colleagues, and champions—all online. Knowledge is everywhere. We just have to seek it.

This unending repository of global knowledge (plus cute kitty and puppy pics, as a bonus) is accessible with a mere click. If we can learn to sift through this plethora of data, be wise in how we glean the gems, and apply what we learn, we'll have more power in our hands than anyone had in the generations before us.

So you have a choice. You can spend your time watching cats playing piano, or you can learn something that will help you get you closer to your aspirations.

The call is yours.

PUT ON YOUR OXYGEN MASK FIRST

Now you may be sitting back thinking this is too much fuss.

You may believe your place has already been defined by your family, workplace, the media, your culture, or your community. Or, you may feel it's irresponsible—especially as a mother and wife—to contemplate your dreams and that it's irrational to make changes in your life right now. You may think it's normal for women to sacrifice ourselves to meet family demands. Besides, when does anyone have the time to dream anyway?

If you believe it's "normal" to put your needs behind others, I'd like to remind you of a time when a majority of the world considered it "normal" to capture inhabitants of coastal West Africa, pack them into the dank bellies of ships and send them across the Atlantic. It was perfectly "normal" at that time to consider the slave in your house an inferior race. It was "normal" to think they were genetically bound to a lower status in society.

This was not that long ago. We now, thankfully, acknowledge how frighteningly absurd and immoral those presuppositions were. We'd never consider this to be "normal" today—not in a trillion years.

In the same vein, I ask you, what presumptions do you hold or allow others to hold of you that prevent you from standing in your own power? What judgments and opinions do you and everyone around you consider to be "normal," but that keep you down?

If you are a mother, an aunt, a teacher, a mentor, or any adult who has young girls around you, you have a responsibility to do the right thing.

If you remain stuck in an unhappy life or worse, maintain harmful behaviors or relationships, you're sending strong signals to these impressionable minds. You're telling them that living a mediocre life is okay. You're telling them that devaluing yourself or putting your needs behind someone else's is perfectly fine. You're telling them it's acceptable to die with regrets, not having made those big, beautiful dreams inside you come true.

You're creating a generation of women who'll know nothing more than unhappiness and hopelessness. And the cycle will continue.

Ask yourself what kind of role model you want to be for the girls around you. What messages are you sending them? If not for yourself, take control of your life for those who love you and look up to you.

Flight emergency announcements ask us to put our own oxygen mask on first, for good reason. It's so we can be prepared to help those around us.

In the same manner, we must take care of ourselves and maintain mental, spiritual, and physical health so we can support and uplift those around us. If we're gasping for air, we're not just harming ourselves, we're also putting others around us in danger.

SO WHAT DO WE DO?

We need to wake up, give our heads a shake and ask ourselves how the way we live impacts our well-being and those around us. Then, we need to find out what we plan to do with this precious and short life we have. Ask yourself what makes you happy, what you wish to do, and what you yearn to achieve.

Find that and follow it until the end.

There's an old saying: *if you don't know where you're going, any path will get you there.* That is, nowhere.

It's crucial that you create your vision and carve your own path in life. If you don't take that first step toward your goals on your own volition, you'll be following someone else's expectations. And other people's demands are never designed to meet your needs.

When we find the courage to uncover our greatest potential and realize our ambitions, we'll also be making a positive impact in the lives of our children, our families, our communities, our country, and perhaps even the world. Yes, even the world.

Never sell yourself short.

Your Rebel Dreams

"There is no greater agony than bearing an untold story inside."
Maya Angelou

WHERE AM I TODAY?

This is your first exercise.

Before we find out where we want to go, we need to understand where we are right now.

Are you, at this moment, living your dream? Or did you stall somewhere in life and are now wondering where it all went wrong? Are you happy and fulfilled, or do you feel drained and empty? How do you feel about yourself, your environment, the people who surround you or the work you're doing when you wake up every morning?

Write down below how you see your life today. Write your answers without thinking too hard and without judgment. This is not how you *should* see yourself or what you *should* be doing. This is merely how you feel today.

Be honest with yourself.

How do you feel about your life today?

1. **My physical health:**

    - Meh. Not feeling anything really.
    - It's bad. Feeling pretty low.
    - Fine. I'm making do.
    - Fantastic!
    - Other: _____

2. My mental state:

- Meh. Not feeling anything really.
- It's bad. Feeling pretty low.
- Fine. I'm making do.
- Fantastic!
- Other: _____

3. My family:

- Meh. Not feeling anything really.
- It's bad. Feeling pretty low.
- Fine. I'm making do.
- Fantastic!
- Other: _____

4. My love life / closest relationship:

- Meh. Not feeling anything really.
- It's bad. Feeling pretty low.
- Fine. I'm making do.
- Fantastic!
- Other: _____

5. My friendships / community:

- Meh. Not feeling anything really.
- It's bad. Feeling pretty low.
- Fine. I'm making do.
- Fantastic!
- Other: _____

6. My career / work environment:

    ❧ Meh. Not feeling anything really.

    ❧ It's bad. Feeling pretty low.

    ❧ Fine. I'm making do.

    ❧ Fantastic!

    ❧ Other: _____

7. My finances:

    ❧ Meh. Not feeling anything really.

    ❧ It's bad. Feeling pretty low.

    ❧ Fine. I'm making do.

    ❧ Fantastic!

    ❧ Other: _____

8. My future:

    ❧ Meh. Not feeling anything really.

    ❧ It's bad. Feeling pretty low.

    ❧ Fine. I'm making do.

    ❧ Fantastic!

    ❧ Other: _____

9. Other_____:

    ❧ Meh. Not feeling anything really.

    ❧ It's bad. Feeling pretty low.

    ❧ Fine. I'm making do.

    ❧ Fantastic!

    ❧ Other: _____

Your Rebel Dreams

Once you're done, turn the page and carry on with the remaining exercises.

When you get to the last page of this book, you can come back and compare what you wrote down here with what you learned, created and envisioned at the end. I bet you'll be surprised!

"I have no regrets. I wouldn't have lived my life the way I did if I was going to worry about what people were going to say."
Ingrid Bergman

DEATHBED REGRETS

Do you know the top five regrets people mention on their deathbeds? A chill went down my spine when I first read this list a year ago.

Top Five Deathbed Regrets, by Bronnie Ware

1. I wish I'd had the courage to live a life true to myself, not the life others expected of me.
2. I wish I hadn't worked so hard.
3. I wish I'd had the courage to express my feelings.
4. I wish I had stayed in touch with my friends.
5. I wish I had let myself be happier.

From *The Top Five Regrets of the Dying* by Bronnie Ware.

Can you imagine coming to this sad conclusion only days before your last breath? That would be hell. An absolute nightmare, one you'd literally never wake up from.

According to Bronnie Ware, a palliative care nurse, people who were terminally ill for long periods usually held resentments as a result of not speaking their minds. Most of their sicknesses came about because they didn't express themselves fully or because they held conflicting beliefs that weren't in tune with their fundamental values.

This means, throughout their lives, they worried about what others thought and engaged in activities that others expected or demanded of them instead of standing in their own power.

"Many did not realise until the end that happiness is a choice. They had stayed stuck in old patterns and habits. The so-called 'comfort' of familiarity overflowed into their emotions, as well as their physical lives. Fear of change had them pretending to others, and to their selves, that they were content, when deep within, they longed to laugh properly and have silliness in their life again." -- Bronnie Ware

Learning this made me obsess about minimizing regrets. I wanted to design a life that was authentic to me, so when I got to the end, I'd have done what I wanted to do and used myself up. All of myself.

Ask yourself how your life is devised. Is it all about meeting the restrictive expectations of those around you—your family, your friends, your community, or your societal traditions? Are you ignoring your own needs, desires, and dreams?

If you are, you may be creating an unhappy and unhealthy life that will lead to a deathbed of regrets.

OUR PAST DOES NOT DEFINE US

But it's not too late to hit the reset button. Our past or present circumstances don't define us. Neither are they an indication of what is ahead of us.

The future lies in our own hands. Our destiny is created by the choices we make today. No matter what has happened in the past, no matter how hurt or harmed we were yesterday or how disappointed or depressed we are today, we can always look forward with hope for a better future—that is, if we have the courage to do so.

Our time on Earth is way too short to not live life to the fullest. Plus, our lives can change in a split second, so do you really want to risk ending up in a hospital bed, or worse, on your deathbed, thinking *if only…?*

"EVERYBODY DIES BUT NOT EVERYBODY LIVES"

Watch this fantastic six-minute video made by Prince Ea, an educator, artist, and songwriter, who says everything I'm saying here but with breathtaking scenery and beautiful music. Watch it every morning and you'll find it a better wake-up call than any espresso shot you'll ever have.

http://youtu.be/ja-n5qUNRi8

Your Rebel Dreams

"Many women live like it's a dress rehearsal. Ladies, the curtain is up and you're on."
Mikki Taylor

HOW MUCH MORE TIME DO YOU HAVE?

Our time on Earth is limited. With every second, we get closer to our end, and we never know when or where or how it will be played out.

All we know for certain is that time slips by every second, and with the loss of each moment comes the loss of an opportunity to live our lives fully. We can duplicate, replicate, lend, borrow, and make money, but we can never do that with time. We can never get time back. Neither can we buy time. The best we can do is make the most of right now.

Would you like to know how many more days you have on this planet?

This calculator was developed by a team of researchers at the University of Pennsylvania. The questions they ask are universal and general enough to be relevant to anyone who lives anywhere in this world, but keep in mind this only provides a general probability, not any certitude, of course.

Go ahead and take this survey, for fun if nothing else, and come back to this book when you're done. Make sure to record your final score.

Life Span Calculator: Visit this website to calculate your life expectancy

https://www.blueprintincome.com/tools/life-expectancy-calculator-how-long-will-i-live/

A. What is your life expectancy from this survey?

Years	

B. What is your age today?

Years	

C. How many years of life do you have left, barring exceptional circumstances (A-B)?

Years	

Highlight, circle, and underline this last number (C).

Even as you read this, your life is slipping away. I don't know about you, but knowing this makes me want to jump up and do something meaningful with my life.

What are you going to do with the remaining time you have on Earth? Will you live intentionally from now on?

OUR INHERENT HUMAN VULNERABILITY

Life can turn on a dime at any moment.

As much as we'd like to believe we're invincible, our physical bodies can be gone in an instant, whether through an illness, an accident, or worse. I learned this recently when someone near and dear to me, someone who was as strong as an ox and in superb health, ended up in a two-day coma after an accident.

It was the day I was shocked into realizing how vulnerable and precious life is. I understood then how important it is to live the life I dreamed of and not waste another minute pretending to be someone else or trying hard to meet other people's expectations rather than my own.

What's stopping you from living a life you won't regret?

Your Rebel Dreams

> *"The bitterest tears shed over graves are for words left unsaid and deeds left undone."*
> Harriet Beecher Stowe

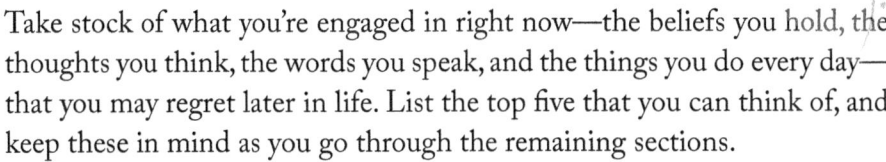

WHAT WILL I REGRET?

Take stock of what you're engaged in right now—the beliefs you hold, the thoughts you think, the words you speak, and the things you do every day—that you may regret later in life. List the top five that you can think of, and keep these in mind as you go through the remaining sections.

What thoughts, words, habits, actions do I have that I'll regret on my deathbed if I continue my life the way it is now?

Thoughts
Words
Habits
Other

Your Rebel Dreams

"Growth is painful. Change is painful. But nothing is as painful as staying stuck somewhere you don't belong."
Mandy Hale

DECISION TRAPS

Like anyone else, I've been guilty.

I've stayed stuck in places I shouldn't have. I've remained with people who brought me down, and I've ignored warnings from my gut. And each time, I paid for it. Badly.

Looking back, I see that every time I made a decision that didn't do me service, it was always because it had been out of tune with my values.

What's interesting is my gut figured this out before my brain kicked in. Every. Single. Time. Now that I've articulated my values clearly and I've also learned to trust my instincts, it's becoming harder and harder for me to fall into the traps of bad decision-making.

Let's pause for a minute and look at the ways we set ourselves to fail in life.

There are four main traps I've seen women, in particular, fall into when making choices. They are: (1) giving in to instant gratification, (2) making sacrifices detrimental to our mental and physical well-being, (3) staying stuck in unhappy places because we fear change, and (4) blindly following scripts handed to us without asking questions.

INSTANT GRATIFICATION

When we drift through life not fully aware of our values, we feel disconnected and discontented. And because we have no clue about who we are, we make decisions to satisfy immediate desires without much thought to how it will impact our lives.

So we reach for that double cheeseburger packed with processed chemicals and dripping in trans fat that will surely clog our arteries. Or we pay for an exotic trip to bring temporary relief to our dull lives when our bank accounts are nearly empty or when we're swimming in debt. And we've all had that friend who can go on a booze-fueled one-night stand with a stranger they've just met, not even thinking of the consequences.

I'm not saying we shouldn't reward ourselves or have fun, but we need to be smart about the choices we make. Otherwise, the consequences of our actions can be harmful, if not debilitating, and that's when we get stuck in life. This is when we give up on our dreams. Because after the fact, after a bad choice is made, we're forced into survival mode, spending all of our time and energy trying to recover from it.

Now, you may say, *"But I don't wanna change. It's too hard,"* or, *"Stop trying to take the fun out of life. I love processed cheeseburgers dripping in trans fats."* That's absolutely your prerogative, but that short-term gain can cost you happiness and the opportunity to have fun for the rest of your life. It's a choice you make.

I know there are environments and situations that are totally out of our control, where we may not have the freedom to make decisions in line with our values. But even in the direst of circumstances, we still have the option of how to respond to that situation, and that alone can have an immensely positive impact on our peace of mind.

If you don't believe me, I highly recommend Viktor Frankl's world-renowned book *Man's Search for Meaning*. It tells an incredible story of how this freedom of choice is possible in any circumstance, even in the monstrous concentration camps of the Second World War.

SELF-SACRIFICE

Self-sacrifice is another unhealthy decision trap we can fall into. I've met so many big-hearted, loving women who live to cater to other people with little consideration of their own values or desires.

They're either conditioned by their families, their communities, or by their own minds to put their needs on the back burner and sacrifice themselves for others—be it their spouses, children, bosses, neighbors, colleagues, place of worship, or that nonprofit where they volunteer.

I know many smart and educated women who work twice as hard and three times as long as their male colleagues, with no rewards in return, simply because they feel it's expected. I know of wives who completely stop their careers to stay home and support their husband's prospects, without a question. I know of mothers who let go of their personal ambitions to spend all their time making their children's wishes come true.

There's nothing wrong with doing things for others, and we, of course, must be there for our loved ones, as they would be there for us. It becomes a problem when we sacrifice ourselves without realizing there are more balanced options to consider. It becomes a problem when we feel resentment building inside us because we're not getting the recognition we deserve for all the hard work we put in, day in and day out. It becomes a problem when we realize we're not living the lives we fully deserve.

The end result is we either become insufferable martyrs or quietly numb ourselves with external stimuli or substances, both of which only make us unhappier. And unhealthier. The conflict that boils inside us in these situations is the kind that will show up one day as a sickness or mental unrest, as Bronnie Ware, the palliative care nurse, found out through her research.

And that's not good.

FEAR OF CHANGE

Some people make bad decisions because they like the easy route. They get on autopilot and do what they're told is the "right thing," simply because it's too difficult to figure out what's truly best for themselves.

For more than a decade, I used to pretend to be someone else, show up every day with a brave smile on my face, work long hours, and not get so much as a pat on my back, just for that biweekly paycheck. I let that paycheck and the title define my worthiness in this world because I was on an autopilot mode that told me "success is to get a couple of degrees, find a well-paying job, and do the nine-to-five for the rest of your life."

That's what everyone else around me was doing as well. Some stumbled and grumbled and buried themselves under monotonous tasks. Others played power games. And almost all hated Mondays. They all dragged themselves to Fridays and then wasted the remaining two days of the week "recovering from work" with either sleep, booze, drugs, or TV. Many did this because they needed to pay for their huge suburban houses, super-sized SUVs, annual exotic trips, and other badly timed decisions.

They were trapped in mediocrity. Cogs for life. Like I was.

I also knew people who worked really hard seven days a week, ignoring their families, children, and health until they got shocked by an illness or divorce. Two of my former colleagues worked like maniacs till their retirement. These were people who told us that they, like everyone else, hated their jobs but were handcuffed by their golden pensions. Both died of heart attacks a few months after they retired.

There are millions of people like this all over the world, people who have voluntarily turned themselves into the living dead, zombies until the day they finally expire their last breaths and die for good.

I lived this life for a long time, thinking this was what I was supposed to do, that it was what society considered successful. I knew I wasn't happy, but change seemed insurmountable.

It wasn't until several life-changing incidents happened all at once, including the accident of a loved one, a chronic illness of a good friend, and a breast cancer scare for me, that shook me to the core and made me realize how much I was punishing myself by working in a toxic environment that kept me unhealthy, physically and mentally.

This was a huge *aha* moment—or year—for me, which helped me embark on a new career and life that are much more aligned with my values.

But it wasn't easy.

I spent a couple of years in serious introspection. I set goals, planned it out, budgeted for it, taught myself new skills, and finally bit the bullet to take my first step into a new career, however scared I felt.

The year I made the shift, my mantra was "feel the fear and do it anyway." I repeated this phrase to myself every day, several times a day. It was what kept me afloat in those times of uncertainty and darkness.

FOLLOWING A SCRIPT

The final decision trap is related to the rules by which we live. The type of scripts that are handed down to us depends on where we live in the world.

In the Western world, the most pervasive and harmful scripts presented to us are about what women "must" look like. If we believe the images and messages that are broadcast by popular media and advertisers today, there's only one ideal body image for all women, and that's an unimaginably undernourished fourteen-year-old girl, photoshopped to the extreme at that.

So, we go around thinking that if we don't look as "flawless" as her, something is wrong with us and we're not worthy of being accepted in society or among our peers. Intellectually, we all know (I hope) this is a ridiculous notion and that women, just like men, come in all sorts of shapes, sizes, colors, and heights, and in that diversity lies beauty. Yet, we take this information in, engrave it into our subconscious from a young age, and surrender to a life of self-hate.

Gail Dines, a professor of sociology at Wheelock College in Boston, said it best: "If tomorrow, women woke up and decided they really liked their bodies, just think how many industries would go out of business."

The good news here is that we have a choice. We can decide what we read and watch and what we expose ourselves and our daughters to. We can decide not to spend our hard-earned money on harmful or useless products that are designed to make us feel bad about ourselves. We can reject these messages and celebrate our bodies as they are. We can learn to prioritize our health over our size, or anything else for that matter.

We already see some change in this space with insightful articles, blogs, books, and documentaries calling out this harmful messaging. There is a growing movement for change. We can do more, but it's a start.

Sadly, things are more insidious in other parts of the world.

Having grown up and lived in different countries, I've met many women who blindly follow rule books for all areas of their lives. From birth to death, their entire lives have been constructed by cultural norms that dictate what they must wear, how and what they must speak, whom they must marry, and how they must behave.

These women, adult women, submit to these codes of conduct without questioning who wrote them or where they came from, conforming to what their society thinks they should do. Many times, those imposing the rules are their own fathers, brothers, husbands, sons or patriarchal community leaders, so they do not dare question them.

Many a time, these women follow these rules even when they are harmful to themselves and their daughters, because the mere thought of standing up to their family or community seems too arduous. And they know the backlash will be severe. So, they shut their minds out of fear and end up living tragic lives.

Several of these women have whispered to me in private that they follow the wishes of others because "it's expected of me," or because "I'm afraid they'll outcast me," or because "it's how its always been done." Some of them worried about getting physically hurt or had already been abused for not toeing the proper cultural traditions expected of them.

The mere fact that anyone would threaten to stop loving you, disrespect you or harm you because you don't follow their commands should send loud alarm bells ringing in your gut.

Only manipulative people who seek to wield power and dominate others play such obnoxious mind games. While you may go about thinking you're being a dutiful daughter or wife, all you're doing is propagating a lifestyle that demeans you. One that demeans all women.

A mother who truly cares for her daughters and desires a healthy and happy environment for them would never permit such destructive practices.

It's time for us all to come to the modern world, where every human being counts, regardless of gender, sexual orientation, race, or other concepts bound by artificial social constructs that only serve the purposes of those who desire to domineer over others.

It's time to acknowledge that, as a woman, you have an equal place in society and that you can make up your own mind, regardless of what your father, husband, brother, culture, tradition, or community or religious leader says.

Yes, it takes a whole whack of courage to shake off a playbook that's handed to you by an entire community, but ask yourself this: is this what you want imposed on your own young daughters?

We didn't progress as a human species by holding on to age-old practices just because "this is how it's always been done." That is a poor and unintelligent excuse given by those who wish to maintain status quo. If we followed archaic traditions by rote, without the necessary critical or analytical thinking they deserve, we'd still be hunting for our food and rubbing stones to make fire.

It's time for all of us to come to the twenty-first century. Stop following scripts and make your own rules for a change!

MAKE A CHANGE

Making change is not easy and it certainly won't happen overnight.

We will need to be mindful of what's going on around us as well as what's going on inside of our minds. We will need to start thinking for ourselves and for those in our care, especially young girls. We will need to question what's handed down to us.

And we will need to be patient with ourselves if we want to get out of our current mindset.

Most importantly, we will need to remind ourselves daily of our personal values and stay true to them. This will help us make the right decisions that will ultimately lead to our long-term health and happiness.

> *"I'd rather regret the things I've done than regret the things I haven't done."*
> Lucille Ball

IT'S NOT TOO LATE

Someone once said *when you don't follow your dreams, someone else will gladly use you to fulfill theirs.* How true. If we allow it, we can become lifelong puppets in someone else's game.

But it's never too late to make the right decisions and change our trajectory. It's never too late to ask the important questions we need to ask.

You can stop at any time and take a different path in life. Stepping out on a new route doesn't require a huge outlay of cash, connections, or coaches. They may help, but in some cases, they may hinder instead.

The only two things you'll need to pack for your life journey are your courage and your resourcefulness, both of which we all have in abundance. We just need to dig inside ourselves to find them.

BUILD YOUR FOUNDATION

Now some of you may be saying, *Gosh, all I want is to lose my muffin top,* or *change my stupid job,* or *get out of this bad relationship. Isn't there a quick magic pill for that?*

Sorry, but magic pills don't exist, and if anyone tries to sell you any, be aware that they rarely work or will come with harmful side effects.

What we need to do is ask ourselves a more important and powerful question.

Before we limit ourselves with short-term goals like losing weight, changing jobs, or any other transient craving that comes clamoring into our heads (especially at the beginning of every new year), we need to do some foundational work. Before we do anything, *anything*, we need to first ask ourselves who we want to be.

Once we answer that fundamental question, the rest will follow through, whether it's a brand-new relationship, a new job, a healthier you or achieving that life-long dream of yours.

Change isn't easy, I know, but once you do this introspection, you'll have a stronger foundation for your life and a map to your dreams. Focus on the life you want to live and all those other things will fall into place, as long as they align with your values and who you believe yourself to be.

FINDING YOUR PASSIONS AND PURPOSE

For most of us, finding our purpose in life or figuring out our passions doesn't come like a thunderbolt from the sky.

It takes time, patience, soul-searching, asking the right questions, and trying new things before we find answers. This workbook is designed to short-cut years of frustration and give you the tools to get to these answers now. This still means work on your part—time, effort, and the courage to dig deep and find out who you really are and what you value.

Most importantly, this requires you to sit up, put your hand over your heart, clear your mind and make a solemn promise to yourself that you are *determined* to go on this new life journey. Make this promise to yourself or you'll remain stuck where you are.

And buckle up, because we're ready to start the ride.

"The biggest adventure you can take is to live the life of your dreams."
Oprah Winfrey

WHAT YOU'LL NEED FROM HERE ON

1. Keep an open mind.

2. Understand that you have choices.

3. Know that your possibilities are endless.

4. Believe in yourself.

. . . AND MOST IMPORTANTLY, ENJOY THE PROCESS.

As you go through the exercises in this book, you may get some jump-outta-your-chair *aha* moments. Or, you may not get all the insights right away. It may take a few tries before you figure them out. Give yourself time, and remember there are no right answers.

The best results come when you respond instinctively. Let your heart speak. Listen to it with love and care, then write down what it says.

You make the best choices given the time and place you're at and the information you have at that moment. It's perfectly fine if you come back to this workbook a year later and see a different path. That's called growth.

WRITE IT DOWN

When you write things down, it gives you more clarity and focus, allows you to think bigger, helps you remember more, and gives you a greater chance of achieving what you want. Writing your thoughts down can even reduce the level of anxieties you face.

Use the white spaces in this book to write all your answers. You'll be thankful you did later on.

LET YOUR ANSWERS PERCOLATE

It's best to follow the topics as they appear, as skipping sections may not give you the full outcome you're looking for. For example, you need to understand what you wish for before setting goals and making a plan. But, at any time, feel free to put this book aside and come back to it later.

When completing this workbook myself, I found the best results came if, after doing one section, I let the ideas swirl around in my brain over a walk, my chores, or supper. Then, when I came back to the exercises, I had the answers I was looking for.

Give yourself time and take all the breaks suggested here.

Most importantly, let the process take its course and have fun with it.

WE'RE ALL UNIQUE

Remember, we're very different from each other.

One woman's life dream could be another's nightmare. Some of us may want to become songwriters or engineers, while others may want to set up their own businesses. Others may wish to travel around the world with their family, seeing wonderful new things. None of these paths are intrinsically good or bad. They're just different.

Your goals are whatever you want them to be.

Comparing ourselves to the Joneses only kills our spirit. It's not only a useless venture but a crippling one. Diversity is what makes this world go around and besides, the seven billion of us can't possibly all want the same thing, can we? How boring would that be?

There's only one of you, and that's who we'll be focusing on and celebrating here.

Your Rebel Dreams

"Begin today. Declare out loud to the universe that you're willing to let go of struggle and eager to learn through joy."
Sarah Ban Breathnach

SET YOUR INTENTION

You can breeze through this entire book in two hours if you want to, but that won't give you the results you are searching for. So, we're going to go through this workbook in sixty days.

Schedule in just one hour per week - every Sunday - for the upcoming nine weeks. Sixty minutes every Sunday afternoon or any other day that's quiet for you is all you need. Think of this as your me-time. Put it in your calendar and make sure others know you need to focus and not be interrupted.

That's nine weeks for you to complete each section, absorb what you learn, take action on new ideas and come up with a vision for yourself that meets all your unique needs and wants.

If you're serious about finding your passions and purpose in life, you will need to mull over your answers, think through your actions and put into practice the lessons you will learn here. Clarifying your life's purpose doesn't happen overnight. For most of us, it takes years, decades even.

So if you're looking for a quick fix, this book isn't for you. Close this book right now and hand it over to someone else. But if you understand that this process will require time and effort on your part, then read on.

Your Rebel Dreams

MAKE YOUR PLAN

We're going to go through this workbook in sixty days.

I suggest you take a week off between each section to let the ideas, thoughts and feelings marinate inside you. Then come back to this book the following week refreshed and ready to move on to the next phase.

Here's your plan.

Week 1 Sunday:

Date:	Complete Section One: My Values

Week 2 Sunday:

Date:	Complete Section Two: My Flair

Week 3 Sunday:

Date:	Complete Section Three: My Zone

Week 4 Sunday:

Date:	Complete Section Four: My Joy

Week 5-8 Sundays:

Date:	Complete Section Five: My Service

Week 9 Sunday:

Date:	Complete Sections Six and Seven: My Vision and My Pledge

If you follow the itinerary shown here, it will give you the time to gain clarity on what you want. You'll build an inquiring mindset to see through any fog that's built up in your life and ask the right questions to push through to the other side without stress.

LET'S BEGIN

Have you got your one hour scheduled in? Have you told everyone this is your me-time?

Great.

Now, find a quiet and cozy spot to curl up in with this book, your favorite cup of tea, coffee, or beverage of choice, and a purple pen. Okay, you can use whatever color pen tickles your fancy, but I find purple ink always gives me a creative edge.

And that's all you need. Plus an open mind, of course.

The journey to achieving your dreams is much easier than you think.

A SHORT MEDITATION

Get comfy. Set your book down, and put aside the cup and pen for a moment. Sit still with both feet on the ground, back straight but soft, arms to your sides, and your body relaxed but alert. Close your eyes.

Now, take five deep and slow breaths. Breathe in through your nose and out through your mouth. Feel your diaphragm expand and contract as you breathe deeply. Concentrate on your breath and feel it coming in and going out.

Make your breaths long and slow. Breathe in. And breathe out. Feel the air coming in through your nostrils and filling your insides. Then feel the whoosh of your breath as it leaves you. Keep breathing slowly, gently, mindfully.

Take your time and take as many deep breaths as you need to settle yourself. This will help you relax physically and clear your mind of any men-

Your Rebel Dreams

tal debris that could cloud your thinking. When you're done with the meditation, sit back and open up to the next page.

Answer the questions that show up, one by one. Be honest with yourself. Indulge in yourself. Put down responses that make you smile. You don't have to fill in all the blanks, only what you want.

You can start each section of this book with this short meditation to get you in the zone. And remember to celebrate every time you finish a section!

WEEK ONE

Let's get to know ourselves better.

SECTION ONE MY VALUES

Values are the foundational building blocks that are the basis of our beliefs, thoughts, desires, decisions, and behavior.

There are ten questions on discovering your values in this section.

Your Rebel Dreams

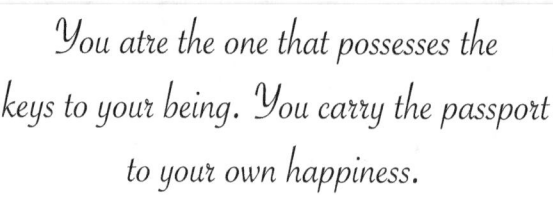

You atre the one that possesses the keys to your being. You carry the passport to your own happiness.

Diane von Furstenberg

PRINT EXERCISES IN BOOK

Download the PDF worksheet booklet for *Your Rebel Dreams*.

This 100+ page booklet includes worksheets for all the exercises in this book. You can print them, write your answers directly on them, pin them up if you'd like and refer to them every day.

Visit the link below to download your free private copy.

https://www.RebelDivas.com/rebel-dreams-gifts/

Your Rebel Dreams

"Here are the values I stand for: honesty, equality, kindness, compassion, treating people the way you want to be treated and helping those in need."
Ellen DeGeneres

MY FOUNDATIONAL VALUES

Values are the building blocks of your life and the framework by which you live.

They make up your inner compass that guides you when life throws you curveballs.

It's your values that help you with the difficult decisions you need to make, especially when you come to forks in the road of life. Understanding your values will give you strength and courage and make it harder for anyone or anything to push you down. Or keep you down.

Self-awareness is one of the hallmarks of a successful person. And the first step here is to reveal what values you hold deep inside.

Learning about your values will teach you what you're made of and what kind of person you are. Most importantly, it will make you more aware of your life's purpose.

So, before you go any further and before you start considering what kind of life partner to look for, what new career to pursue, or even how much weight you want to lose, you'll need to discover your fundamental personal values.

Then, you'll find that aligning everything you do with your values is the easiest way to effect change—all those challenging adjustments you know you need to make. This is also the best way to make those changes stick in the long term, and is what will give you a fulfilled life, one where you thrive, not just survive.

Turn the page to discover who you really are.

> *"One is not born, but rather becomes, a woman."*
> Simone de Beauvoir

MY VALUES QUESTION 1

Okay, let's start by describing yourself. What are your five strongest characteristics?

These could be physical, intellectual, personality-driven, or other traits you feel truly personify you. Write them down in the space below.

Here are four interesting (and free) character tests, each of which takes about five to eight minutes to do. I found the results to be very close to how I see myself. They also showed little deviation from the results of expensive human resource tests I've done as part of career growth programs at my various corporate workplaces.

If you're having a hard time answering this question, take one or more of these self-assessments before you fill out the list below.

- Character Strength Survey:
  http://www.viacharacter.org/www/Character-Strengths-Survey
- My Personality Test:
  https://my-personality-test.com
- Personality Test:
  https://www.123test.com/personality-test
- 16 Personalities Test:
  https://www.16personalities.com/free-personality-test

What are my top five character traits?
1.
2.
3.
4.
5.

> "Connection gives purpose and meaning to our lives."
> Brené Brown

MY VALUES QUESTION 2

What type of people do you admire the most?

This could include teachers, neighbors, family members, celebrities, activists, artists, even characters in movies or novels. Write down at least the top three people—fictional or real, dead or alive—who inspire you.

And if you can, write down next to each person why they inspire you. Is it because they're honest and show integrity? Is it because they're doing incredible work you'd love to do yourself one day? Or is it because they have gorgeous hair and drop-dead good looks?

These answers will reveal a lot about who you are and what you value most. Write them down without judgment.

1. Who do I admire?
Why they inspire me:

2. Who do I admire?

Why they inspire me:

3. Who do I admire?

Why they inspire me:

4. Who do I admire?

Why they inspire me:

5. Who do I admire?

Why they inspire me:

> *"Your success and happiness lies in you. Resolve to keep happy, and your joy and you shall form an invincible host against difficulties."*
> *Helen Keller*

MY VALUES QUESTION 3

Think about a time when you felt truly joyful. What was going through your mind, and what were you doing when you felt that way? Write down the top five times in your life when you felt ecstatic. Then, if you can, write next to that why you felt so good.

1. What makes me happy?

Why this makes me happy:

2. What makes me happy?

Why this makes me happy:

3. What makes me happy?

Why this makes me happy:

4. What makes me happy?

Why this makes me happy:

5. What makes me happy?

Why this makes me happy:

> *"Stress is an alarm clock that lets you know you're attached to something not true for you."*
> Byron Katie

MY VALUES QUESTION 4

Can you think of a time when you felt overwhelmed, stressed out, or even angry?

When we're upset, it's a clear signal things are out of whack, and most of the time, we're in an environment that does not align with our values. So what stresses you out? What makes you puff up like the Hulk? Let's capture these triggers so you can be aware of them and know what to avoid and when.

Write down the five things or environments or people that made you really unhappy recently. If you can, write next to that why you reacted the way you did.

1. What upsets me?
Why this upsets me:

2. What upsets me?

Why this upsets me:

3. What upsets me?

Why this upsets me:

4. What upsets me?

Why this upsets me:

5. What upsets me?

Why this upsets me:

> *"In the beginning, people think vulnerability will make you weak, but it does the opposite. It shows you're strong enough to care."*
> Victoria Pratt

MY VALUES QUESTION 5

Can you think of a time when you felt vulnerable? The occasions you felt defenseless and naked say a lot about who you are.

Write down below those times when you felt most exposed or unprotected. If you can, write next to that why you felt that way. This question may bring out emotions of fear or sadness in you, but don't resist them. Allow them to wash over you. Acknowledge them. Thank them. Then answer the question.

Remember, being vulnerable never means you're weak or that you have anything to be ashamed of. Not by any means. Not by a million miles. It's merely an emotion like any other, a useful one that teaches us about ourselves and those around us.

Here's a beautiful quote by Brené Brown, a researcher and professor at the University of Houston and an expert on human vulnerability:

"Owning our story can be hard but not nearly as difficult as spending our lives running from it. Embracing our vulnerabilities is risky but not nearly as dangerous as giving up on love and belonging and joy—the experiences that make us the most vulnerable. Only when we are brave enough to explore the darkness will we discover the infinite power of our light."

1. What makes me feel vulnerable?

Why I feel this way:

2. What makes me feel vulnerable?

Why I feel this way:

3. What makes me feel vulnerable?

Why I feel this way:

4. What makes me feel vulnerable?

Why I feel this way:

5. What makes me feel vulnerable?

Why I feel this way:

"Define success on your own terms, achieve it by your own rules, and build a life you're proud to live."
Anne Sweeney

MY VALUES QUESTION 6

How do you define success?

Remember, both Mother Theresa and Richard Branson are considered highly successful, but their visions and their work couldn't be more different. Both took immense risks and neither conformed to what their environment or societies told them to do.

We all define success differently.

For some, it could mean the richness of their relationships with friends and family or the number of people they impact in the world, or it could be the amount of free time they have. For others, it could be the amount of money in their investment portfolios, the size of their home, or the price of their cars or clothes. Put down what's important to you without judging.

Let's define success in our own terms, not based on what others tell us.

How do I define success?

How does this idea of success make me *feel*?

> *"I am a woman of substance. Don't judge me by my looks, my clothes or the way I wear my hair. . . I have the capacity to endure pain and survive despite all the odds in my life because I am strong through and through. I'm unique in my own special ways even with my flaws and imperfections. I am proud of what I am."*
> — *Aarti Khurana*

MY VALUES QUESTION 7

What would you never sacrifice for even a billion dollars?

This could include people, relationships, mental prowess, physical looks, health, or status. Don't think of what you should say, write down what you feel is right for you.

Think of the things or people you consider to be the most important to you, that you couldn't bear to lose for all the money in the world. And if you can, write down next to each item why you wouldn't sacrifice that thing.

1. What is priceless in my life?
Why this is priceless to me:

2. What is priceless in my life?

Why this is priceless to me:

3. What is priceless in my life?

Why this is priceless to me:

4. What is priceless in my life?

Why this is priceless to me:

5. What is priceless in my life?

Why this is priceless to me:

> *"Just don't give up trying to do what you really want to do. Where there is love and inspiration, I don't think you can go wrong."*
> — Ella Fitzgerald

MY VALUES QUESTION 8

What would you do if you had only nine months to live?

Imagine, if you will, as macabre as it sounds, a visit to your doctor, who tells you in a deadpan voice that you have only nine months to live. That's it. That's all. How would you feel? What would you do if you had less than a year left on this planet?

The top five things I would do if I had only nine months to live starting today:

1. What I'd do:
Why this is so important to me:

2. What I'd do:

Why this is so important to me:

3. What I'd do:

Why this is so important to me:

4. What I'd do:

Why this is so important to me:

5. What I'd do:

Why this is so important to me:

> *"Fame and success and titles stay with you, but they wear out eventually. In the end, all that you are left with is your character."*
> Ana Ivanovic

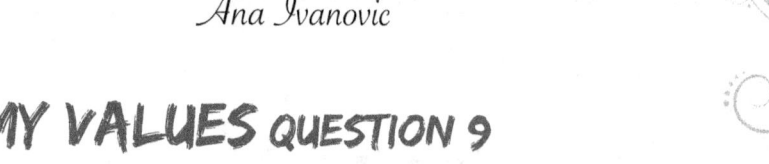

MY VALUES QUESTION 9

What would you want your friends and family to say about you at your funeral?

Imagine yourself walking into a funeral parlor room. Everyone you know is here, dressed in mourning attire. There's a beautiful wooden casket in front surrounded by wreaths and flowers. When you walk up to it, you're startled to find your own body inside.

"Ahem." Someone behind you clears her throat. You turn around. It's your best friend, and she's asking everyone to take a seat as the ceremony is about to begin. Then, she asks anyone who wants to say a few words about your life to stand up and come forward. Who will stand up, and what will they say?

Who will speak about me at my funeral, and what would they say?

1. Who:
What they would say:

2. Who:

What they would say:

3. Who:

What they would say:

4. Who:

What they would say:

5. Who:

What they would say:

> *"Don't compromise yourself. You are all you've got."*
> Janis Joplin

MY VALUES QUESTION 10

Imagine a white marble stone that will stand at the head of your grave for eternity, announcing to the world what your life was about in a handful of words. Write down what you'd like to see on that tombstone of yours.

Here lies:
Who has:

> *"Life's ups and downs provide windows of opportunity to determine your values and goals. Think of using all obstacles as stepping stones to build the life you want."*
>
> *Marsha Sinetar*

MY VALUES PULLING IT ALL TOGETHER

Now, take fifteen quiet minutes and go back to the beginning of this section. Mindfully read the answers you gave to each of the questions on your values.

You've captured a pretty good picture of what's most important to you, who inspires you and what impact you want to leave behind on your loved ones. Keeping all this in mind, you should now be able to identify at least three to five core values that are most precious to you.

Here's your next exercise.

The next page has a list of common values, but it is not exhaustive. Highlight those that resonate with you the most or come up with your own. Suspend judgment and don't think too hard. Choose what comes to your mind first and list your top values below.

Don't second-guess yourself here. The words that jump out to you are usually the most relevant answers.

My core values:

1.	4.
2.	5.
3.	

Abundance	Family	Philanthropy
Accuracy	Fitness	Politeness
Adventurousness	Fortune	Positivity
Affection	Freedom	Power
Altruism	Friendship	Preparedness
Ambition	Fun	Rationality
Athleticism	Gratitude	Recognition
Authenticity	Happiness	Relaxation
Beauty	Harmony	Reliability
Bravery	Health	Reputation
Calmness	Helping society	Resourcefulness
Charm	Honesty	Respect
Collaboration	Humbleness	Sacrifice
Commitment	Humility	Science
Compassion	Independence	Security
Conscientiousness	Individuality	Self-control
Consistency	Information	Sensuality
Courage	Integrity	Sexiness
Creativity	Intelligence	Sharing
Curiosity	Justice	Solidarity
Determination	Knowledge	Solitude
Diligence	Leadership	Spirituality
Directness	Liberty	Spontaneity
Donating	Love	Teaching
Efficiency	Loyalty	Trustworthiness
Empathy	Maturity	Truth
Endurance	Mindfulness	Valor
Energy	Nature	Vitality
Equality	Optimism	Wealth
Faith	Perfection	Wisdom
Fame	Perseverance	

> *"Courage is the price that life exacts for granting peace."*
> Amelia Earhart

ARE YOU LIVING YOUR VALUES TODAY?

Now that you've identified your foundational values, sit back for a few minutes and really think about how they define your character and your personality.

Are you living true to your values, or have you fallen into any of the decision traps outlined in the previous pages? Is your life based on your own values or someone else's?

If you find yourself constantly unhappy or depressed or feel that life has not turned out the way you wanted, it might be a good indication that your life is in conflict with your fundamental values.

THE DIFFERENT SHADES OF VALUES

I've shared only positive values in the previous list, but we all know values come in various shades and shapes.

History has shown us how tyrants, from Adolf Hitler to Idi Amin, acted upon their abhorrent personal values, leading to widespread destruction of millions of innocent people. The world is, unfortunately, not rid of such evildoers yet. Many countries still struggle with basic human rights issues today.

Other more common negative values include dishonesty, selfishness, laziness, cynicism, pessimism, disrespect, manipulation, and jealousy, among others. Do you recognize these in yourself or others around you?

Having held some of these values in my early life and having lived with people that had these negative values in the past, I've seen how these attitudes can create destructive habits.

People with negative values are consumed by their dark feelings. Some of them know full well the hurt they inflict on others, but are so selfishly closed off to the world, they don't have an iota of understanding of the pain they're causing. The one commonality among them is how they wallow in their darkness, rife with mental torment and physical sickness, even if they don't show this to the outside world.

So, we have a choice of what kind of values we want to hold, given what kind of life we want to live. We need to think about how we want to treat others and how we want to be treated in return.

These aren't insignificant questions to ask ourselves.

FIND YOUR BOUNDARIES

There's an awesome side effect to understanding our values. It makes it much easier for us to create and maintain our personal boundaries.

Our boundaries tell us how far we allow others to intrude into our sacred physical and mental spaces. When we embrace our values, we send a clear signal to others where our boundaries lie and how far they can push us. Most importantly, this also means we know when to say no.

Many of us go through life agreeing to any request that comes our way simply because we fear being rude, because we don't want to miss out on something, or because we're aimless and have no guidance on what to accept or not.

We, women, especially tend to say yes with a pretty smile on our faces, because we're too afraid of offending others. When we say yes to everything, we often find ourselves regretting it, and eventually resenting ourselves for being doormats.

Now that you have a better understanding of your values, you'll find it easier to overcome this problem. While it may take some practice at the beginning, you'll find the right reasons to say a polite, yet firm "no" when and where warranted.

The other positive side effect here is you'll start to feel really good about yourself when you stand up for your values.

SHARE YOUR VALUES

I made a decision a few years ago to share my values with the world on my website.

Writing my values down and broadcasting them reinforced them even further in my psyche. I'm also held accountable by everyone now. If I veer from my values, others will surely notice, and some may even speak up. This means I keep them at the top of my mind and always ask myself if I'm thinking, speaking, and behaving true to my own personal values.

The second reason I share my values is because that tells others I stand for something, that I have principles. It says I don't seek validation from others or allow external forces to tell me what to do. It shows others that I have a backbone and that I'm content simply by being me. And this is a powerful place to be.

Don't be afraid to share your personal values with those around you. You'll soon find the respect others have for you will grow. They'll begin to understand you better and will have no choice but to acknowledge you as you are.

And this is the path to becoming a Rebel Diva.

SO, HOW DO YOU FEEL?

That's the end of this section. Write down anything that wasn't captured in the questions but that you want to get out of your system or share on paper.

1. How do you feel after completing this section?

- ○ Meh. Nothing interesting here
- ○ I really want to get this, but I'm lost and need help
- ○ I'm doing well. Just need to think some more
- ○ Fantastic. I've nailed this round. Woo-hoo!
- ○ Other: _____

2. Where do you still need to figure things out more?

A.

B.

C.

3. What actions will you take in the next seven days to keep this topic on the top of your mind and clarify it further?

A.

B.

C.

BREAK

See, that wasn't too hard, was it?

Self-awareness is nothing to sneeze at, but it's not rocket science either. This is worthwhile work—digging deep into yourself, so you can start living a life of no regrets.

Now it's time for a break. Put a bookmark on this page and close the book.

Why not reward yourself by doing something nice? Make yourself a cup of tea or coffee and have it with your favorite treat. Take the kids to the playground, or get out and watch the sunset with your fur babies in tow. They're waiting for you.

Enjoy your break. See you next week.

> *"Never underestimate the power of passion."*
> *Eve Sawyer*

OUR PASSIONS

I'm a big believer in embracing our passions.

If you listen to anyone who has become successful, they will tell you the first step of their journey was to discover their passion. Their second step was to follow it with zeal and focus.

As far as we know, we only have one life to live. So, why sacrifice our blood, sweat, and tears to build up someone else's dreams? Why stay small and hide our passions under a pile of anxieties and worries?

Following your passion is not only the joyful and meaningful thing to do, but it is passion that will keep you going when things get rough, as they invariably do in life. Passion is what will help you persevere when it feels hard to take just one extra step. If you love what you do, you will keep walking no matter what's thrown at you.

Now, I know some people who think passion is fluff. To them I say, at least I will have tried to do what mattered to me. I will have done what moves me, what makes me sing and fills me with joy. So, on my deathbed, I can smile to myself and say, I gave it a go. *I lived.*

FINDING PASSION

So, how do we find this elusive thing called our passion?

How do we figure out what brings us joy every day so we can live to our fullest potential?

Here's what I learned over the past decade of asking these very questions. After a lot of introspection, reading a mountain of books and articles, and talking with self-development gurus, life coaches, teachers, and friends who were going through a similar exploration, and through my own personal experience, I discovered that our passions lie on a crossroads.

This crossroads is the junction of four important areas of our life: what we're good at doing or can learn (flair), the environment in which we thrive (zone), what we love to do (joy), and what the world needs (service).

So, here it is—the passion equation:

> **My Passions = My Flair + My Zone + My Joy + My Service**

Let's break this down.

My Flair - Flair is what you do well. These are your talents and what you're typically good at. This includes the skills you've worked to improve, as well as what you're able and willing to learn in the future.

My Zone - Zone is the physical environment in which you live and work, the people you surround ourselves with, and the information you listen to, watch and absorb every day.

My Joy - Joy comes from what you love doing. These are the things that make you jump out of bed in the morning, eager to start the day. Joy alone is not worth pursuing if you don't have the other areas figured out.

My Service - Service is what value you can give to others or what you offer to the world. This is a need in others that you can fulfill with your talents and skills. For many of us, this is where our purpose lies and where our why kicks in.

My Circle of Values - All these areas need to be encompassed within your core value set; otherwise, it won't make sense to pursue any of them. You always need to live true to your fundamental personal values.

A HOLISTIC VIEW

Now, you may be shaking your head wondering, "Why the heck do I need to think about all these areas?" You might think all you need is the "joy" part of this equation and you'll be set for life.

Very few people, if any, have done work they enjoy doing, snapped their fingers and made their dreams come true. While it may look like that from the outside, the truth is a bit more layered.

There are some people who appear to have gone on to success despite their level of skill or their environment or the value they gave to others. If you look closely, though, you'll see they always found a way to gain the necessary knowledge along the way, to shut out negative environments, find focus among chaos and give what the world wants, so they could follow their passions in the long run.

But what if we can make this path of discovery easy for us?

What if we can reverse engineer this process from the beginning so we minimize the pitfalls people normally fall into? What if we incorporate all these areas and plan our days, energy and effort *intelligently*, so we're not muddling our way through the dark?

Let's set ourselves up for success, not failure.

WHY WE STRUGGLE

When I see people who are struggling in life or are unhappy, it's usually because they've only fulfilled one or two of these areas, or sadly, none of them.

Joy alone won't sustain you for long. If you enjoy doing something but you don't have the talent or the skill to do that task, or you can't make a living off it, you'll end up getting frustrated.

Having flair—talent or skill—alone won't satisfy you either. Working well on a passionless task will only make you feel hopeless, which is, sadly, where a majority of us find ourselves today.

The world is full of diligent people who mean well. They work very hard for their paycheck, but end up feeling dissatisfied. Making money may give you a temporary payoff and is necessary to meet your basic needs, but it can also leave you feeling hollow if your soul is running on empty.

Having joy and flair alone will not help either. We all probably know of that one artist friend who loves what they do and does it beautifully, but lives under a hazy cloud of poverty, certain the world doesn't care about their art. But they haven't taken the time to ask how their work could be of value to others, or how they could communicate their gifts to the world as a service. Some artists do this very well, but they are rare.

The trick is to find the crossroads where all these areas intersect—what brings you joy, what you're good at and can learn, the environment best suited for you, and the value you can offer others. This is what will make you feel fulfilled and sustain you in the long run.

To find your ideal passions, you'll need to explore all these areas of your life.

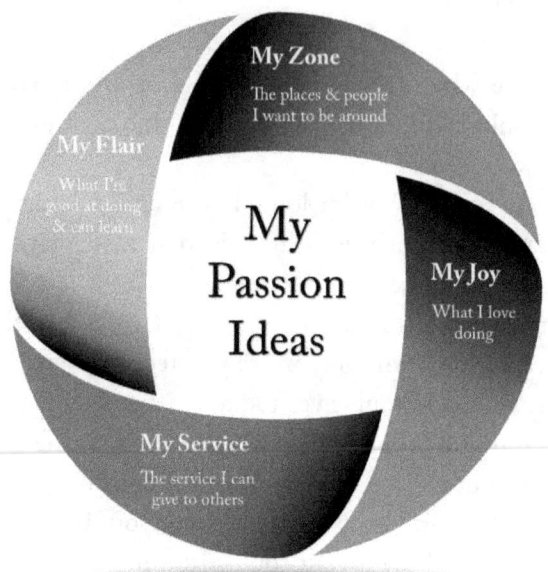

My Circle of Values

WHAT'S NEXT

This workbook will take you by the hand through each of these areas. You will find easy-to-follow exercises designed to help you identify your flair, your zone, your joy and your service. Once you are done with these individual exercises, you will put it all together to reveal the intersection where your passion ideas lie and create a vision for yourself—a vision that will make your dream life come alive.

This work will require reflecting on your part, and you will need to write your thoughts down in the spaces provided here, but that is a necessary part of your self-discovery journey.

Knowing where all your different needs fit in this picture will help you design a holistic and happy life that's in tune with your values. This will stop you from becoming another zombie who stumbles through life. You will discover your energy and joy again. You will pursue work that makes you feel alive. You will look forward to every day.

The side effect to all this is you will be walking toward the dreams you wish for in life. The journey will be well worth it.

Your Rebel Dreams

WEEK TWO

Let's find out what we're good at.

SECTION TWO MY FLAIR

Flair is what we do really well and what we're capable of learning and improving (which is ultimately limitless).

There are six questions on identifying your talents and skills in this section.

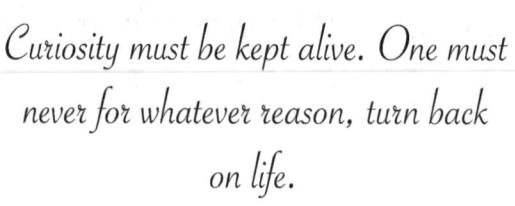

Curiosity must be kept alive. One must never for whatever reason, turn back on life.

Eleanor Roosevelt

"Nothing in life is to be feared. It is only to be understood."
Marie Curie

MY FLAIR QUESTION 1

This is the first question in your quest to find your innate talents.

Have you ever been so engrossed in a task that you forgot everything else and the world melted away around you? When have you found yourself so immersed in something that time slipped away and you didn't even notice? What were you doing when you felt that way?

Think through these questions and answer below. Choose the first memories that come to mind as they're usually the right ones. Remember,

The times when I get fully engrossed in the task at hand are:
1.
2.
3.
4.
5.

Your Rebel Dreams

we're seeking our personal truths here, not what we should be doing or what others tell us we should be doing.

> *"I know what I want. I have a goal, an opinion. . . and love. Let me be myself and then I am satisfied. I know that I am a woman, a woman with inward strength, and plenty of courage."*
> *Anne Frank*

MY FLAIR QUESTION 2

Now, let's make an experience inventory of your life to date.

Think of all the things you are proud of creating or doing, even if no one else noticed or said a word.

Write down the main jobs or projects that you did well. This work could have been at the office, at home, at school, in your community or at an event. Don't think about the titles you had or the income you received, but focus more on the type of work you were doing and how well you did it.

Each of the questions below focuses on one area of your life. If they're not relevant to you, scratch the bold words out at the end of each question and add your own.

1. Jobs/tasks/projects I did well **at work**:
Why I did this work so well:
A
B
C

2. Jobs/tasks/projects I did well **at home**:

Why I did this work so well:

A

B

C

3. Jobs/tasks/projects I did well **at school**:

Why I did this work so well:

A

B

C

4. Jobs/tasks/projects I did well at _____:

Why I did this work so well:

A

B

C

> *"Never limit yourself because of others' limited imagination; never limit others because of your own limited imagination."*
> Mae Jemison

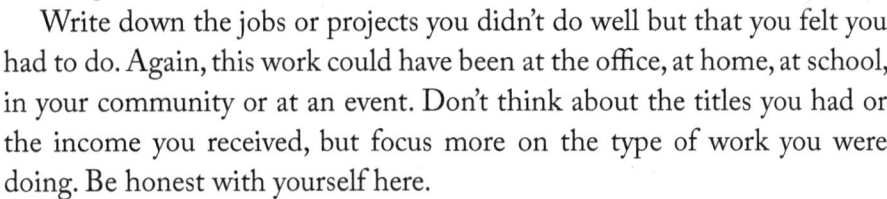

MY FLAIR QUESTION 3

Let's flip this around now.

Write down the jobs or projects you didn't do well but that you felt you had to do. Again, this work could have been at the office, at home, at school, in your community or at an event. Don't think about the titles you had or the income you received, but focus more on the type of work you were doing. Be honest with yourself here.

By identifying the tasks you didn't do well, you can consciously eliminate activities that don't inspire joy in your life. If you think this question is not important, think of all the people you know who do work they hate day in and day out, every day of their lives. How happy are they?

Can you imagine what it would be like to live an entire life like that? What do you think they'll be whispering to themselves on their deathbed?

1. Jobs/tasks/projects I didn't do so well **at work**:
Why I didn't do this work so well:
A
B
C

Your Rebel Dreams

2. Jobs/tasks/projects I didn't do so well at home:

Why I didn't do this work so well:

A

B

C

3. Jobs/tasks/projects I didn't do so well at school:

Why I didn't do this work so well:

A

B

C

4. Jobs/tasks/projects I didn't do so well at_____:

Why I didn't do this work so well:

A

B

C

"You can't be that kid standing at the top of the waterslide, overthinking it. You have to go down the chute."
Tina Fey

MY FLAIR QUESTION 4

What do you do that gets you the most compliments?

Have you received congratulations, awards, accolades, ribbons, medals or positive reviews for something you enjoyed doing? List them regardless of how small or large the recognition was. This can be work done at the office, your home, or even a place you volunteer on weekends.

Don't restrict yourself or judge the appreciation you received. Now is not the time to be humble.

The most important (to me) recognitions I've received are:
1.
2.
3.
4.
5.

> *"I never dreamed about success, I worked for it."*
> Estée Lauder

MY FLAIR QUESTION 5

What do you know more about than anyone else? What do your friends and colleagues call you for when they need your help?

Make an inventory of your top areas of knowledge. This could be anything from sewing to baking to real estate law to aerospace engineering—and anything in between. Write these down without judgment.

Next to your list, write down where you garnered this knowledge. You don't need to have had a formal education in the field. You may have learned this skill by yourself or by watching someone else. You may have gained the knowledge through a training program, a college course, a degree or even by simply watching a video online.

Put all this down to help jog your memory and capture as many of your major knowledge areas as possible. If you want to add more than five, go right ahead.

My top knowledge areas:

1
Where I gained this knowledge from:

2

Where I gained this knowledge from:

3

Where I gained this knowledge from:

4

Where I gained this knowledge from:

5

Where I gained this knowledge from:

"You get whatever accomplishment you are willing to declare."
Georgia O'Keeffe

MY FLAIR QUESTION 6

Imagine you're walking into the most important interview of your life to get that dream job you've always wanted. After the initial chitchat and warm-up questions, the interviewer sits back, looks you straight in the eye, and asks what your biggest accomplishment has been to date.

You can name a project you recently completed or talk about how you got promoted at work. But as someone who's sat on both sides of the desk and has interviewed hundreds of applicants for jobs, I can tell you what impresses everyone the most is when someone gives an emotionally captivating story from their personal life.

Examples could be how you cared for a loved one struggling through a chronic illness, or how you overcame one yourself. Perhaps you had a challenging childhood where you were forced to be caretaker and mentor to your younger siblings. Maybe you gave your time and energy to volunteer for a community in distress halfway around the world. Or you did something modest to help someone out, but that small act of kindness made an immense impact in their life.

These are the stories that showcase hidden talents inside of you and show others what kind of person you really are. These are the stories you'll remember on your deathbed and that will make you smile. Share those.

We all have these experiences tucked away, uncelebrated, undistinguished. If you search inside yourself, you'll be sure to find examples, many of them even. It's time to let them out and shine.

So what do you consider to be the greatest accomplishments in your life to date?

1. My greatest accomplishment:

Why this is important to me:

2. My second greatest accomplishment:

Why this is important to me:

3. My third greatest accomplishment:

Why this is important to me:

> *"The most common way people give up their power is by thinking they don't have any.*
> — Alice Walker

MY FLAIR – PULLING IT ALL TOGETHER

Now take ten minutes and flip back to the beginning of this section. Read all the answers you gave here while thinking about your innate talents. After going through these questions, you should have a good idea of what these might be.

Examples could be:

- Performing arts and theater
- Working with disabled kids
- Negotiating legal agreements
- Leading a team
- Running a marathon
- Baking cookies
- Anything that comes to you from this exercise

Now, write down your top talents below.

We're only taking stock of where you are right now to get an indication of where you're starting. But remember, you never, ever want to restrict your dreams to what you know or are good at today. There are infinite possibilities for you to learn and grow in many directions tomorrow—some of which may still be hidden, and which we'll uncover in the next Rebel Diva book when we plan your path toward your vision.

The things I'm really good at doing and what I consider to be my innate talents are:
1.
2.
3.
4.
5.

SO, HOW DO YOU FEEL?

That's the end of this section. Write down anything that wasn't captured in the questions but that you want to get out of your system or share on paper.

1. How do you feel after completing this section?

- ○ Meh. Nothing interesting here
- ○ I really want to get this, but I'm lost and need help
- ○ I'm doing well. Just need to think some more
- ○ Fantastic. I've nailed this round. Woo-hoo!
- ○ Other: _____

2. Where do you still need to figure things out more?

A.

B.

C.

3. What actions will you take in the next seven days to keep this topic on the top of your mind and clarify it further?

A.

B.

C.

BREAK

Outstanding work.

The questions you went through, while simple, went deep within you and may not have been easy to answer at first. But if you took the time to reflect and write your answers down, you're heading closer to achieving your life's dreams.

Now close this book and go celebrate the hard work you've done in this section.

While you're on your break, let your mind wander to other things. Your brain will subconsciously reflect on what you've been writing, and you'll come back to the next stage of this workbook with a fresh mind, brimming with energy and new ideas.

Enjoy your break! See you next week.

Your Rebel Dreams

WEEK THREE

Let's find our ideal environment.

SECTION THREE MY ZONE

Zone is the physical environment in which we live and work, the people we surround ourselves with, and the information we absorb every day.

There are four questions on understanding your optimal environment in this section.

If you just set out to be liked, you would be prepared to compromise on anything at any time, and you would achieve nothing.

Margaret Thatcher

"When dealing with critics always remember this: Critics judge things based on what is outside of their content of understanding."
Shannon Alder

MY ZONE

Look around you.

What kind of people do you live, work, and hang out with every day? What kind of information do you feed your mind on a daily basis? What kind of physical environment are you immersed in every day? Is it a healthy or harmful one?

Your environment, or zone, can make or break you.

If you're surrounded by people who have unhealthy lifestyles, hold negative thinking patterns, or who have never attempted anything productive and show no success in any areas of their lives, how do you think that will impact your life?

You can have everything figured out about yourself, your values, your desires, and your talents, but if you're surrounded by jealousy, criticism, laziness, or constant complaining, you're going to struggle. It will be like swimming against the current in a raging river. You'll have to work very hard to keep your head above the water.

Your environment can support you in your swim to success, or drag you down and drown your dreams.

The places you live and work, the people who surround you every day, the things you hear, see, read, and watch are all an indication of how successful your life will be. So, it's really important to consciously choose the surroundings that will foster your growth and happiness and help you stay at your very best.

MAKE THE SHIFT

Jim Rohn, one of the most influential motivational leaders of our time, said famously, "You're the average of the five people you spend the most time with."

But of all the shifts you will want to make, this may be the hardest. Changing your environment won't be easy, especially if the people closest to you—family and friends—are not aligned with your values.

But what's your alternative?

They say a baby eagle who grows up among chickens will never realize the heights to which it can soar. Whenever the eaglet flaps its beautiful wings and tries to fly, the chickens give it mocking looks and ask, "Who are you to fly?" or, "Stop being so silly, we're chickens, we don't fly." An eagle who lives in that environment will never know any better and will die never having soared in the open blue sky. What a sad life would that be?

So you will have to decide whether to stick with the chickens on the ground scratching dust, or to fly out and soar to meet other eagles like yourself.

TRUST YOUR GUT

This is one area of my life where my instincts have played a phenomenal role. Whenever my gut warned me about someone I'd just met and I ignored the feeling and continued to engage with that person, I always regretted my decision. It's taken some time, but I've learned to trust my gut, and am much happier for it.

If you're unsure how to choose the right people whom you allow into your inner circle, listen to your instincts. Your gut may know the right answer faster than your brain does.

Remember though, there's a difference between your instincts and your fears.

You may feel a tinge of nervousness when you're meeting a well-meaning mentor or high-profile leader in your field for the first time. This is quite different from the red flags your stomach sends you when you meet someone whose values are diametrically opposed to yours, or who may even mean you harm.

By staying in the moment and being mindful of every engagement, you'll start to notice the difference and know when to withdraw quickly and when to move forward with confidence.

BE SELECTIVE

Now, I know it's easy to talk about creating an environment with the right people, but it's hard to do because we get distracted and preoccupied by what others think or say about us. But, what would your life be like if you lived without one smidgen of worry about what others think?

The truth is, most people are too busy being absorbed in themselves. They're not thinking about you as much as you think they are. When anyone judges you, it's most often a reflection of their own limitations, fears, and how they perceive the world. It's not a reflection of you.

I cannot count how many times I've been given unsolicited "advice" from finger-wagging people who felt it their place to tell me what to do. This includes friends, relatives, colleagues and even people I'd just met. Every time I bumped into such people, I walked away feeling like I'd been pecked to death by a broody chicken.

Now, I'm not talking about the constructive criticism and wise advice from true mentors who genuinely want the best for me. I'm talking about the naysayers—the "little people." These are the folk who are quick to dismiss ideas and clamor loudly to tell me what won't work with no evidence to back up their claims.

Interestingly, once I ask a few questions and dig a bit deeper, I find these "little people" know much less than I do and are more lost than I am. They always disappear once they know I'm on to them.

It took me a while to realize one other very important lesson.

The size of someone's house, the price of their car, or their company title has little correlation to their *life* success. It is those with the greatest debt, the biggest problems, and the most unhappiness in life who are also the most eager to tell me how to live mine.

So, be aware.

It's wise to be selective about who we get advice from and who we surround ourselves with. And when I talk about "other people," that includes me.

Please don't take anything in this book as gospel, because it's not. These are life lessons from my own experiences and a lifetime of hunting for knowledge through my eyes. Not everything here may be relevant to your situation.

Use this guidance wisely, tailor it to your circumstances, and use only what will help you to progress to your dreams.

"I just love bossy women. I could be around them all day. To me, bossy is not a pejorative term at all. It means somebody's passionate and engaged and ambitious and doesn't mind leading."
Amy Poehler

MY ZONE QUESTION 1

Look around you and ask yourself these questions:

- What kind of people do I spend the majority of my time with?
- What are they like?
- How do they see the world?
- Are they people I can look up to, learn from, and emulate?
- Do they make me feel good inside, or do I feel bad every time I hang out with them?
- Do they lift me up when I'm down, or do they bring me down?
- Do they support my goals or do they make fun of them?
- Do they treat me with respect or do they treat me badly?
- Are they patient and compassionate, or are they quick to anger and dismiss me?

Now, take stock of the five people you spend time with the most.

1 Who?

What's their personality like?

How do they encourage and support my success?

2 Who?

What's their personality like?

How do they encourage and support my success?

3 Who?

What's their personality like?

How do they encourage and support my success?

4	Who?

What's their personality like?

How do they encourage and support my success?

5	Who?

What's their personality like?

How do they encourage and support my success?

Your Rebel Dreams

> *"Surround yourself with the right people, and realize your own worth. Honestly, there are enough bad people out there in the world—you don't need to be your own worst enemy."*
> Lucy Hale

MY ZONE QUESTION 2

Now, let's change the conversation around. What kind of people do you want to surround yourself with?

Les Brown, a motivational and public speaking legend, has a mantra that reads, "Only Quality People." OQP for short. I added an "H" to that to come up with OHQP. Allow only high-quality people into your life, people who share your outlook on life, who lift you up, support your ambitions and treat you with respect.

On the next page are examples of personal characteristics of OHQP. Highlight those that resonate with you the most, or write down your own ideas in the space below.

MINI MEDITATION

If you're having a hard time doing this exercise, here's a small tip. Do a ten-minute visioning exercise, where you imagine yourself in an environment you enjoy.

Set a timer for ten minutes. Then, sit comfortably and close your eyes. Take five deep breaths in and out.

Now, let your mind wander to a place you enjoy being in. This could be your home, school, work, gym, a party, a networking event, a conference, a community center, a restaurant, an outdoors hike, on top of a mountain, on a boat in a river, or on an exotic trip.

Imagine the people you want to surround yourself with in this place. See yourself mingling, talking, laughing, and connecting. Linger here. Tune out of your brain and go into your heart. Feel the inspiration that you get from these people around you. Go deeper and stay there until the timer rings.

Take five slow, deep breaths and gently open your eyes.

Now answer this question.

The kind of people I want to surround myself with are:
1.
2.
3.
4.
5.

Here are examples of positive people to invite into your life:

- Accepting of differences
- Action takers
- Adaptable
- Adventurous
- Appreciates diversity
- Balanced
- Believers
- Brave
- Bright
- Calm
- Caring
- Champions
- Cheerleaders
- Compassionate
- Confident
- Considerate
- Content
- Courageous
- Courteous
- Creative
- Curious
- Empathetic
- Empowering
- Encouraging
- Energetic
- Enthusiastic
- Excited about life
- Fair
- Fearless
- Fit
- Frank & honest
- Friendly
- Fun-loving
- Funny
- Generous
- Gentle
- Grateful
- Happy
- Hardworking
- Healthy
- Holistic
- Honest
- Idea generators
- Imaginative
- Independent
- Inspiring
- Intelligent
- Supporting justice
- Kind
- Leaders
- Masters in their fields
- Nice
- Open-minded
- Optimistic
- Original
- Passionate
- Peaceful
- Philosophers
- Positive
- Rational
- Reliable
- Resilient
- Risk-takers
- Role models
- Secure
- Self-disciplined
- Self-reliant
- Social leaders
- Straightforward
- Strong
- Strong-minded
- Successful
- Supportive
- Teachers
- Team players
- Thoughtful
- Trustworthy
- Warmhearted
- Winners
- Wise

> *"One's philosophy is not best expressed in words; it is expressed in the choices one makes. . . and the choices we make are ultimately our responsibility."*
> Eleanor Roosevelt

MY ZONE QUESTION 3

We're not just greatly influenced by the people around us, but also by the activities we engage in every day.

Here are a few questions to ask yourself before you answer below:

- How do you spend most of your time on any given day?
- Do you like to spend time on social media or watching television?
- What videos do you like to watch and what podcasts do you like to listen to?
- Do you like to read? If so, what books, articles, or newspapers do you prefer reading?
- What courses, seminars or learning activities do you try out every week?
- How many hours in a day do you consume entertainment?
- Are the conversations you engage in typically about other people or are they about ideas?

Your Rebel Dreams

The top five things I do on a normal day are:

1

How helpful this activity is for my personal growth:

2

How helpful this activity is for my personal growth:

3

How helpful this activity is for my personal growth:

4

How helpful this activity is for my personal growth:

5

How helpful this activity is for my personal growth:

> *"Courage is like a muscle.
> We strengthen it with use."*
> Ruth Gordon

MY ZONE QUESTION 4

Think about the amount of time you spend at work on any given week.

For most of us, work consumes more than a third of a day. So shouldn't we try to ensure that environment is congruent with our values? It's when our values aren't aligned with our work environment that we begin to hate our jobs, complain about our colleagues, and come home feeling drained.

Let's take stock of all the different factors of our work surroundings, one by one.

For example, for time of day, you may prefer working later in the day because that's when your productive juices start running, and the thought of waking up early and dragging yourself out of bed makes you cranky.

It's good to identify these things up front, so when you put everything together later in this workbook, you can look for the right workplaces that best meet your unique personal needs.

So, what does your ideal work environment look like?

1. What **time of day** do I like to work?

2. How many **hours a week** do I want to work?

Your Rebel Dreams

3. Who would I like to have **control over my schedule?**

4. Who would I like to have **control over the work I do?**

5. How do I like **learning** new things?

6. Do I need someone to give me direction, or **do I prefer working for myself?**

7. Do I want to work **independently** or in a **team?**

8. Do I need my teammates physically close by, or can **I work remotely with others?**

9. What **tools or equipment** do I like to use at work?

10. What **level and kind of noise** do I like or can tolerate when at work?

11. What **level of lighting** do I like when I work?

12. Do I like disarray and a **mess or a clean** and uncluttered space?

13. Do I want to work in **one place or travel** extensively for work?

14. What does the **physical space** I like to work in look like?

> *"We are products of our surroundings."*
> *Amber Valletta*

MY ZONE - PULLING IT ALL TOGETHER

Take ten minutes now, go back and read the answers you gave for the exercises in this section.

Then, look at your current environment and ask yourself where you'd like to see changes. This is not going to be an easy exercise, and you may feel emotional when doing this, but it's important to be honest with yourself here.

IDENTIFY YOUR "I'M FINE" AREAS

Mel Robbins, a phenomenal motivational speaker and author of the *5 Second Rule*, says the most misused four-letter word in the English language is *fine*. "I'm fine" is the most common response given by people when asked how they're doing. According to Mel Robbins, this word is a cop-out. It's a polite and quick way to make yourself and others believe everything is okay, so you don't have to make difficult changes.

If you are truly living a happy life, one that's in tune with your values in an environment that cherishes and champions you, you'd jump up to say, "I'm doing great!" with a dazzling smile. Not "I'm fine" with a tepid shrug.

Many people hide their passions and live a mediocre life because they don't want to rock the boat. They're worried about being rejected or anxious about being judged by those around them. Even if they know they've got to change their environment, they don't want to make the effort to make the shift.

So they justify their inaction by saying, "Things are fine," but you can see the lack of life in their eyes. Most people who are stuck in a rut will never even meet your eye because they know they're living a lie and they don't want you to see it. They don't want to see it themselves.

I was one of those people who used to give that noncommittal "I'm fine" for years. When I broke out of that environment and started doing the work I love, things changed drastically. Now I can't stop talking when someone inquires how things are going. I'm learning to tone it down a bit so I don't scare my friends off, but I walk around every day with a grin on my face.

Even if you may not feel like making the changes you put down below write it all out anyway. By doing so, you'll have a record of what matters to you. After that, taking action will become much easier.

So, what changes do you want to make in your environments?

1. What I'd change in my **personal** environment:

Why I need this change:

2. What I'd change in my **family** space:

Why I need this change:

Your Rebel Dreams

3. What I'd change in my **learning/educational** space:

Why I need this change:

4. What I'd change in my **work** place:

Why I need this change:

5. What I'd change in my **friendship** circles:

Why I need this change:

6. What I'd change in my **volunteer** places:

Why I need this change:

7. What I'd change in my _____:

Why I need this change:

SO, HOW DO YOU FEEL?

That's the end of this section. Write down anything that wasn't captured in the questions but that you want to get out of your system or share on paper.

1. How do you feel after completing this section?

- ○ Meh. Nothing interesting here
- ○ I really want to get this, but I'm lost and need help
- ○ I'm doing well. Just need to think some more
- ○ Fantastic. I've nailed this round. Woo-hoo!
- ○ Other: _____

2. Where do you still need to figure things out more?

A.

B.

C.

3. What actions will you take in the next seven days to keep this topic on the top of your mind and clarify it further?

A.

B.

C.

BREAK

You're done with this section. Good for you.

Did you find the exercises here challenging or were they a breeze? Either way, it's important to give your mind a rest now and let your brain work in the background. This way, you can digest your answers and come up with more ideas.

Now close this book and go celebrate the hard work you did.

Enjoy your break! See you next week.

> *"Find something you really care about and mix that with something you love doing."*
> Kathleen Hanna

I grew up an angry child, furious at the world.

My childhood home was rife with emotional torment, and I never knew what the next day would bring. Because my family moved constantly, I had no one to confide in and no mentors to look up to, so I turned into a lonely and sullen young woman who believed the world was against her.

I blamed everyone, was mad at everything, and got myself physically ill. I was a miserable human being for a long time. Trust me, you did not want to be around my younger self.

It took decades of digging into myself, learning to love myself and forgive others, before I found the calmness and clarity I desperately needed. Through this self-reflection, I learned how to transition out of unhappiness and anger and find happiness in life.

WHAT I DISCOVERED ABOUT HAPPINESS

Here's what I found out about happiness.

First, I realized that happiness is a personal choice, not something you search for outside of yourself.

Second, I recognized that happiness, as cliché as it sounds, is a journey, not a destination.

Third, I learned that happiness is this amazing combination of being in the moment, feeling grateful, and living a meaningful life.

Brendon Burchard, speaker, trainer, and author of the *Motivation Manifesto* (an impressive book, by the way), says happiness is not something we "discover." It's not something we come across by happenstance or a goal we strive toward. Happiness is something we are able to generate every day, just like a power plant generates electricity. It's an internal mechanism that's entirely within our control.

This is the most important lesson I've learned about happiness—that we can do something about our unhappiness. How empowering is that?

It's within our power to change how we feel, no matter what's going on around us. We can decide to wallow in sadness and misery, which only invites more of that into our lives, or we can decide to wake up and be happy that day.

So, it's up to you to make the choice to look at the world in a different light and think the thoughts, speak the words, and engage in the behavior that will bring you happiness and joy.

I know some of you are shaking your heads by now, wondering, "You just think yourself happy? C'mon, seriously?"

Before you throw this book out the window, I want to say you're correct. Thinking happy doesn't just happen naturally, and yes, changing unhappy thoughts takes time and energy. There is no magic switch for happiness, at least as far as I know.

Here's what I do know.

We, humans are, by nature, geared to automatically grasp at negative thoughts. We're built to worry impulsively and be anxious about our surroundings and our future.

This was a survival mechanism when the saber-tooth tigers roamed the Earth and is the result of a primitive brain trying to protect us in the most efficient way it knows how. But in our modern world, these worries, anxieties, and such negative emotions hinder rather than help.

It takes effort to push down negative triggers that spontaneously spring to mind, and it takes energy to switch to more progressive and positive thinking patterns. What we need to do is engage the modern part of our brain as much as possible and try our best to respond intelligently versus react in knee-jerk fashion.

If you're wondering if this effort is worth it, let me share a tidbit with you.

Have you heard the myth that successful people are happy people? In reality, it's the other way around. Happy people are the ones who succeed. People who make the choice to be happy create the right juices inside them that help them do well in life.

Isn't that good news?

The even better news here is we have the power within us to become happy, and this should feel empowering. Super empowering.

HOW TO CREATE HAPPINESS

So, how do we go about generating happiness?

Let me share with you the happiness equation that has helped me increase the level of joy in my life exponentially.

I learned that whenever I'm mindful of my thoughts, words, and deeds throughout the day, or whenever I'm feeling grateful for what I have, or when I'm living with intention and purpose, I find more joy and contentment. Combining all three areas really ratchets up these good feelings, so I've come up with the happiness recipe below.

> Happiness Recipe = Mindfulness + Gratitude + Purpose

Let's break this formula down a bit.

MINDFULNESS

Mindfulness means enjoying the moment.

It's the realization that this second is all we have. Ruminating about the past is futile. Even elephants can't drag yesterday back. Agonizing over "should haves" and "would haves" will only give us migraines. Worrying about the future is just as unnecessary—a self-inflicted torture, really. Mark Twain once said, "I've had a lot of worries in my life, most of which never happened." How true.

Right now, this very second is all we have in which to do what we wish. So let's make the best of it. Now isn't that inspiring—knowing we have control over our state of mind?

Mindfulness is not just empowering, it can be joyful.

You'll find that out when you take the time to focus on what you're doing, whether you're watching a sunset or that hummingbird hovering over a flower in your garden, or concentrating on a hobby you love. It's these small moments that create happiness in our lives.

When we're fully engaged in the now, even if it's as unpleasant as being at the dentist (with apologies to dentists everywhere) or in a traffic jam, studies have shown, over and over again, that being in the moment is freeing and creates a positive mental state.

GRATITUDE

Gratitude means being thankful for what we have right now.

Every time I've sulked over what I didn't have or what I hadn't achieved, it was a surefire way to become unhappy, frustrated and stressed out. When we brood, we're only encouraging more of those negative emotions to come our way. Instead, when we focus on appreciating what we already have, it opens the doors to more abundance. More of the good stuff.

I've also learned that gratefulness can't live in the mind at the same time as anger or sadness or resentment. So, whenever you want to change your mood and bring more happiness to your day, look around you for the things you are grateful for. Your emotional well-being will uplift almost immediately.

Gratitude has one more amazing side benefit. Feeling thankful for what we have opens our hearts to greater compassion. When we feel grateful, we see the many things or people or places or experiences which we may have taken for granted before.

Whenever I feel blue, I remind myself how millions of women in poverty around the world live today, and how lucky I am in contrast to them. Just realizing this makes my selfish sadness vanish into the night. It also makes me eager to do more to help my fellow sisters around the world and motivates me to keep doing what I do—which, in turn, increases the level of joy in my life.

PURPOSE

Of the three areas that bring happiness, purpose may be the most difficult to figure out.

Simon Sinek, an author and one of the most respected thought leaders of today, says we must always start with our why. I don't think this applies only to the business world; it is just as, or even more important in our personal lives.

Our why is what drives us. It's knowing who we are, what motivates us, and why we do what we do. In short, it's a reflection of our foundational values.

Finding our purpose is knowing our why. Living our purpose is spending each moment with intention and aligned with our values.

You're already well on your way if you completed the previous section on values in this book. When you live every day with these intrinsic values on top of mind, it becomes harder for you to drift aimlessly, to stay stuck in a rut, or follow a script handed to you.

When you find your purpose, it becomes more difficult for others to push you down and keep you down. In fact, it raises the respect others have for you, and you gain credibility in their eyes. Most importantly, it gives you a greater sense of self-worth and self-respect. You'll start to live an authentic life, one that matters, one that you can look back on in your last days and smile.

Imagine a life that's fully tuned to who you are and what makes you happy. Just imagine.

Throughout the exercises here, you'll have space to write down why you chose the answers you did. If you want to take full advantage of this workbook, always write down why you answered the way you did. It may take a little longer, but it will help you to validate your authentic purpose.

Make the most of yourself by fanning the tiny, inner sparks of possibility into flames of achievement.

Golda Meir

WEEK FOUR

Let's find what brings us joy.

SECTION FOUR MY JOY

Joy is what we love doing and what makes us jump out of bed in the morning, eager to start a new day.

There are eight questions on discovering your joys in this section.

Your Rebel Dreams

> *"Anyone who has spent any time in space will love it for the rest of their lives. I achieved my childhood dream of the sky."*
> Valentina Tereshkova

MY JOY QUESTION 1

When you were nine years old, what did you say you wanted to be when you grew up?

I believe our childhood minds knew more about ourselves than we do now as adults. As we grow older, we're so conditioned by society, rules, traditions, and what others expect from us that we forget what we're really like.

So, let's go back to our childhoods for a few minutes. Let yourself become a child once again. Now, start dreaming. And dreaming.

What I wanted to become when I was a child:

> *"What a wonderful life I've had! I only wish I'd realized it sooner."*
> Sidonie-Gabrielle Colette

MY JOY QUESTION 2

What do you daydream about as an adult? Where does your mind drift to most often now?

Let your mind wander a bit right now and see where it goes. It might be trying to tell you something.

What I daydream about most often:
1.
2.
3.
4.
5.

"I was smart enough to go through any door that opened."
Joan Rivers

MY JOY QUESTION 3

What do you love to do in your spare time?

Why is it that we spend most of the day on things we don't enjoy and rush back home to do the things we love in the remaining few hours? What if we can turn this around and make what we love doing the priority in our lives?

This will take some serious thinking, planning, and action, but it's absolutely possible and worth it.

What I love to do in my spare time:
1.
2.
3.
4.
5.

"Forget about the fast lane. If you really want to fly, just harness your power to your passion."
Oprah Winfrey

MY JOY QUESTION 4

When have you felt the most authentic? What situations or environments make you feel like you can be yourself?

At my previous day job, which I didn't love, I created a persona that I thought was expected of me in my role—a persona I saw recreated by everyone above me. I felt dispirited and disempowered every day I walked into that office because I was forcing myself to be someone else. This sucked my energy and drained my happiness, to the point the lanyard for my electronic name tag felt like a noose choking me. It took me a long time to realize this grave mistake.

I finally found I could be my most authentic self when I'm working on the things I'm passionate about. I'm now at a place where I can be me, and my productivity, energy, and happiness have all skyrocketed.

So figure out where you can be you, and your journey toward your dreams is halfway done.

When I can be my most authentic self:
1.
2.
3.
4.
5.

> *"If you obey all the rules, you miss all the fun."*
> Katharine Hepburn

MY JOY QUESTION 5

What are you curious about? What do you obsess about? What topics make you sit up and become animated? What ideas do you seek out when you read books, blogs, and articles? What kind of movies, videos, or documentaries do you like to watch?

When someone talks about a subject they're passionate about, their eyes invariably light up and shine, and you can feel the good energy emanating from them. It's a joy to see this happen, but most people never explore this feeling further. And this is how dreams die.

Let's take stock of your true interests without judgment here.

1. What interests me the most:

Why this interests me:

2. What interests me the most:

Why this interests me:

3. What interests me the most:

Why this interests me:

4. What interests me the most:

Why this interests me:

5. What interests me the most:

Why this interests me:

> *"I want a life that sizzles and pops and makes me laugh out loud."*
> *Shauna Niequist*

MY JOY QUESTION 6

What would you do if you had all the resources and time in the world, and you didn't have to worry about money? What would you gladly do for free?

When you're ready to do something without even thinking about the compensation you should receive, you're well on your way to finding the thing you have a passion for.

1. What I'd do for free:

Why this is important to me:

2. What I'd do for free:

Why this is important to me:

3. What I'd do for free:

Why this is important to me:

4. What I'd do for free:

Why this is important to me:

5. What I'd do for free:

Why this is important to me:

Your Rebel Dreams

> *"Don't be afraid of failure; be afraid of petty success."*
> *Maude Adams*

MY JOY QUESTION 7

What would you do if your success was guaranteed? What would you do if you had no fear at all?

One of the most irrational fears many of us have is the fear of failure. This is such a debilitating problem that most of us don't take the first step, even a baby step, toward what we want to do. But what if failure was not an option? What if failure didn't exist and you could do anything you wanted?

1. What I'd do if I were to never, ever fail:

Why this is important to me:

2. What I'd do if I were to never, ever fail:

Why this is important to me:

3. What I'd do if I were to never, ever fail:

Why this is important to me:

4. What I'd do if I were to never, ever fail:

Why this is important to me:

5. What I'd do if I were to never, ever fail:

Why this is important to me:

> *"How wonderful it is that nobody need wait a single moment before starting to improve the world."*
> *Anne Frank*

MY JOY QUESTION 8

If you had all the power in the world, what would you want to change?

Think of Mother Theresa, Martin Luther King, Jr., or Nelson Mandela. Their passions arose from wanting to change the status quo and help the most marginalized people in their communities. Perhaps you have a thirst to change something in this world of ours. You may be yearning to make a difference in your country, your city, your village, your community or even your family.

Our strongest passions come from the things we want to be different—the things that get us all heated up.

1. The changes I'd make if I had all the world's power at my fingertips:

Why this is important to me:

2. The changes I'd make if I had all the world's power at my fingertips:

Why this is important to me:

3. The changes I'd make if I had all the world's power at my fingertips:

Why this is important to me:

4. The changes I'd make if I had all the world's power at my fingertips:

Why this is important to me:

5. The changes I'd make if I had all the world's power at my fingertips:

Why this is important to me:

> *"Joy is prayer; joy is strength; joy is love; joy is a net of love by which you can catch souls."*
> Mother Teresa

MY JOY – PULLING IT ALL TOGETHER

Now sit back, get comfortable, and read the answers you gave in this section. Savor each word and linger on each answer.

Do you see common threads in the answers you gave? Do some topics come up again and again? Does any one of your answers jump out and make your heart leap? If it does, this is the work that will bring you the greatest joy. This is what you'd do even if no one paid you for it.

It's important, though, to not prejudge any of your answers. It's easy to fall into the trap of thinking, "But I'd never find work doing that," or "No one will hire me to do that." This is one of the biggest mistakes people make at such a critical juncture, when they're almost at the finish line.

Contrary to popular belief, the world is full of opportunities for those who are ready to follow their dreams and work hard at their craft. There are flower arrangers, yoga instructors, hypnotherapists, photographers, and plumbers making high six, even seven-figure incomes. There are athletes and musicians making multi-millions.

These successful people have all walked their own path. They are the rebels, not just for the sake of being one, but because they had a dream which they believed in and embraced. Most importantly, they believed in themselves. So they put all their focus and effort into that one idea to become world class at what they love doing.

In contrast, I have some lovely friends with post-doctorate degrees from good universities who barely make a living. I also have friends who have gone to even better schools and make great salaries now but are drowning in debt.

The one commonality among these dear friends of mine is they all followed what someone else expected them to do, whether it was their parents, family, or society. They work very hard at their jobs, but they're not happy and it shows in their lifestyles.

If you take nothing else from these workbooks, take this: follow your own joy.

So, what brings you joy?

Is it dog walking? Write it down. Is fighting deforestation in South America what calls out to you? Put it down. Is helping kids in inner-city schools what makes you feel thrilled? Write it down without judgment. And if it is to become the first female head of state in your country, for heaven's sake, write that down!

Put down all the ideas that pop into your head as you reread your answers to the questions in this section. If your list is long and diverse, don't worry. We'll prioritize them in the coming exercises.

What are the joys you have in life? Answer with abandon.
1.
2.
3.
4.
5.

SO, HOW DO YOU FEEL?

That's the end of this section. Write down anything that wasn't captured in the questions but that you want to get out of your system or share on paper.

1. How do you feel after completing this section?

- ○ Meh. Nothing interesting here
- ○ I really want to get this, but I'm lost and need help
- ○ I'm doing well. Just need to think some more
- ○ Fantastic. I've nailed this round. Woo-hoo!
- ○ Other: _____

2. Where do you still need to figure things out more?

A.

B.

C.

3. What actions will you take in the next seven days to keep this topic on the top of your mind and clarify it further?

A.

B.

C.

BREAK

Awesome work. Did you have fun? I hope so. You deserve a break.

Close this book, and do something that will help you relax.

While you're unwinding, your mind will be busy reflecting on all the things you wrote in this section. This subconscious thinking will bring up even more ideas and answers and prepare you for the next step in this quest to becoming a Rebel Diva.

Enjoy your break! See you next week.

Your Rebel Dreams

Tikiri

WEEKS FIVE-EIGHT

Let's find out what value you can give to the world.

SECTION FIVE MY SERVICE

Service is the value we give to others or what we can offer to the world.

There are four questions in this section on discovering how to give value to others through your passions.

Your Rebel Dreams

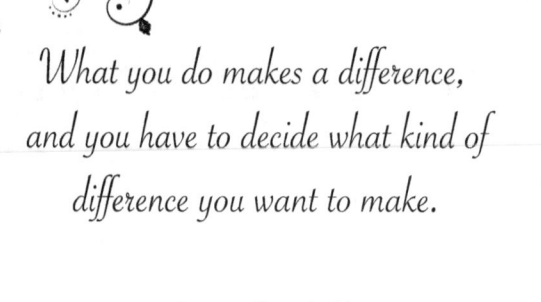

"What you do makes a difference, and you have to decide what kind of difference you want to make.

Jane Goodall

"Life-fulfilling work is never about the money. When you feel true passion for something, you instinctively find ways to nurture it."
Eileen Fisher

FIND YOUR TRIBE

You're probably wondering by now, "This is all well and good. I know what environments I like to live and work in, what talents I have and what I love doing. But how in goodness heck am I going make a living doing work I love? You can't be serious!"

After traveling the world and back and having met many people who do diverse jobs, I can say with confidence there's space on this planet for every kind of work under the sun. The trick is to identify what value you offer others and who will most want what you give. Then you'll need to determine the most suitable language and channels to communicate that value to the right people in the right place at the right time.

No matter what field or industry you're in, whether you want to be an entrepreneur or an employee, you can find a group of true fans who'll find value in the work that brings you joy.

In his blog and book, entitled *1,000 True Fans*, Kevin Kelly says you don't need millions or even tens of thousands to want your work. You only need a small group of people who're just as crazy keen as you are on the topic that brings you joy.

These are the folk who will be sure to collaborate with you, buy from you or hire you. If you're looking for work as an employee, all you really need is to find that one company or organization that's as passionate as you are on your topic.

There are seven billion people on this planet today and many millions of businesses. I'd be surprised if you couldn't find a thousand other human beings who have the same interests as you do.

The mistake many people make is to think they need to serve the entire world through their work in one go. That's the fastest way to get overwhelmed and give up too quickly.

In the end, you may very well serve the world. Think J.K. Rowling with her Harry Potter books, but even she started off targeting her books to a very small niche of young boys. She withheld her first name and used initials on her book covers so potential buyers wouldn't realize they were written by an older woman, which could have turned those discerning young men off. And now, almost everyone regardless of gender and age has read at least one of her books or watched one of the films.

When you're starting out, it's important to hone your ideas to a narrow niche. Pick your best idea and follow that.

Once you win the hearts and minds of a small group of people from that one thing, you'll find others will come calling, and you can expand your vision from there.

MY EXPERIENCE

Before pursuing my own joy of writing novels, I talked to as many readers as I could. I asked a ton of questions to see if there was an intersection between what I wanted to write about and what they wanted to read about.

I researched the kind of writing that appeals to specific groups of readers. I looked up what readers are willing to pay for and how much. I looked at where and how they buy books. It took months to make these connections and get answers, but this homework was well worth my time. Though I also learned not everyone will like the stories I write, I found my tribe of 1,000 fans.

While I was doing this research, I was also fine-tuning my craft. I wrote every evening after work. I shared my stories in writers' circles, took writing and marketing courses at the local college, and met with storytellers and beta readers to get feedback and improve any way I could.

All that hard work paid off. Over time and with many mistakes and a few U-turns along the way, I learned how to share my work with the right people in the right forums and in the right language.

What about you? Are you ready to put some time into searching how your joy can serve others?

AN ITERATIVE PROCESS

The questions in this section are meant to start your thinking. You will need to talk to people and do more research. This is an iterative process where you'll refine your answers as you learn more about your new field of work and start taking action.

As you talk to more people and take a few steps forward, you'll get a better idea of your ideal audience and the value they're looking for. As you get more feedback from your audience, you can adjust the service or product you're creating or the job you're seeking.

Take this one step at a time. As they say, Rome wasn't built in a day. You're building something far more important to you: your future life.

If you're in love with your idea and believe in your future dream, this exploration will be truly enjoyable. It'll be like going on a treasure hunt to find the path to your dreams.

Are you ready?

> *"There is a stubbornness about me that never can bear to be frightened at the will of others."*
> — Jane Austen

MY SERVICE QUESTION 1

Let's see if you can translate what you've learned so far into a discernible service that brings value to others.

The best way I can explain what you'll need to do next is with an example.

Let's take a fine artist—one of those careers almost everyone thinks is doomed to fail—and see what value their work can provide different audiences.

AN EXAMPLE

There was a time when fine artists would wait patiently (starving as they did) to be discovered by a stuffy agent or a patron who'd rent their art to galleries and charge a huge commission—that's if they were lucky. Many artists still wait for rare lightning strikes like this, because that's how it was "always done."

I have a dear artist friend with amazing talent who creates the most breathtaking images on canvas. His work is so detailed and so brilliantly constructed, yet he has difficulty selling his art.

His attempts at nabbing an agent who'll get him "discovered" have been futile for years now. He constantly complains that no one appreciates art anymore and that anyone who's doing well in the art world has sold out. So when he calls, I take him out for a beer so he can drown his sorrows.

But there's a growing number of innovative artists who no longer depend on historically unreliable approaches to make ends meet.

A block down from my artist friend is a team of three young painters who have decided not to wait to be discovered. They don't even try to find an agent. Instead, they convinced a tech-savvy high-school student to help them (for very cheap) and created an online market for themselves, starting from scratch. When they call me, I go to celebrate yet another sale or yet another success by opening a bottle of wine.

No amount of trying to convince my dear artist friend to follow his younger compatriots seems to work. That is truly sad.

These days, there are a hundred and one ways to connect with people from many places via our ever-expanding communication channels. The role of the "middleman," or that agent in the center who'd acted as a gate-keeper and took a chunk of change from your pocket, is becoming less and less relevant. Now, you can offer value directly to the person who wants it, when they want it and where they want it. And in many cases, they could be across the globe.

An artist can reach out to luxury house buyers who want unique art pieces for their new homes. They can connect directly with corporate interior designers who are always on the lookout for art to showcase in corporate headquarters, hotels, conference halls, and other business interiors. I know of small municipalities in my part of the world who seek artists to create one-of-a-kind murals to improve their urban environments.

Then there are people who seek prints, postcards, and posters on online stores like Etsy.com, Amazon.com or Ebay.com. These are platforms where lower-priced art can be sold to many individual buyers anywhere in the world. Think about the fad for coloring books that were selling like hotcakes online, making very good money for their creators.

Selling art is one way to make money. Teaching it is another.

There are retired folks who spent most of their lives in stifling corporate environments who are now itching to discover their creative selves. They'd pay very well, and happily so, for expensive art seminars and private one-on-one courses.

Another option is to connect with online game creators and transfer physical art into the electronic world. Art on canvas could be converted into three-dimensional designs using 3D printing. There are many other ways of incorporating a digital element into art to wow the crowd that seeks innovation and fusion of different areas. An artist can now more easily seek these people out, forge new partnerships and expand their art into whole new markets.

They could look at unconventional collaborations such as science and art, or social justice and art, and see what interesting money-making avenues can be pursued there.

There are many ways an artist can give value to others who'll appreciate their creative work. They just have to do the research, talk to people, and be open to possibilities beyond the conventional.

YOUR TURN

Can you apply similar ideas to the work you want to do?

You could make this more fun by inviting a small group of your closest friends over, serving tea and cookies, and asking them to help brainstorm this question with you. Make it an idea party!

Then, when you're ready, answer this question.

What value can I offer to others from the work that brings me joy?

If you have identified several areas of joyful work, you may want to pick the one you find most interesting today. If you're having a hard time making a choice, do this exercise for all of the areas and we can prioritize them later.

Try to be as clear as you can on the value you will offer and how your target audience will benefit from what you're planning to give them.

1. What I can offer:

To whom:

How they will benefit:

2. What I can offer:

To whom:

How they will benefit:

3. What I can offer:

To whom:

How they will benefit:

4. What I can offer:

To whom:

How they will benefit:

5. What I can offer:

To whom:

How they will benefit:

Tikiri

> *"A boat is always safe in the harbor, but that's not what boats are built for."*
> *Katie Couric*

MY SERVICE QUESTION 2

Once you figure out what value you can give to others through your work, the next step is to better understand your audience—the person or group of people or organization you're prepared to give value to.

You already came up with a quick answer to this in the last question. It's now time to flesh that out. Pick the one offer that interests you the most from your answers to the previous question and rewrite it here. Remember to pick what interests you the most, not what you *should* pick.

What I can offer:_____

To whom: _____

How they will benefit:_____

UNDERSTAND YOUR AUDIENCE

Your audience could come in the form of a client if you want to become a consultant. They could be a customer if you're creating a product or want to get into sales. They could be an organization or a certain manager you

183

want to work for. When you are an employee, your immediate supervisor is usually your most important client.

The best way to understand your audience better is to create an avatar that defines the ideal person who'll benefit from what you're offering.

You can start by answering the questions below. Your answers will, of course, depend on your work and the industry you want to be in, so make sure to add more relevant questions as needed and ignore those that do not apply to you.

Later on, as you experiment and test your idea, you'll review and update this avatar. But we all need to start somewhere, so start here for now.

Try to be as specific as you can about this audience avatar. If you can see them in your mind's eye, you've got it.

When you focus on one person or one organization, you can tailor your message and what you offer to them far more readily than if you have a fuzzy idea of who they are. Being highly specific at the beginning will move you further along on your mission than if you try the scattergun approach and attempt to target everybody.

Remember, you can always expand your reach later on (just like J.K. Rowling did!).

So, what does your ideal audience member (client/colleague/customer/manager/organization etc…) look like?

My ideal audience avatar:

1. Gender (if relevant):

2. Age (if relevant):

3. Physical attributes (if relevant):

4. Family status (if relevant):

5. Languages (if relevant):

6. Location:

7. Education:

8. Occupation:

9. Income:

10. Community involvement:

11. Leisure activities:

12. Main viewpoints:

Your Rebel Dreams

13. Their values:

14. Personality traits:

15. Purchase habits:

16. Social media presence/engagement:

17. Other:

"My journey continues because I've conquered a lot. And I know how to conquer the rest."
Mary J. Blige

MY SERVICE QUESTION 3

Now that you have an idea of the value you can offer others and what your ideal audience avatar looks like (for now), you can take this one step further. You can get more clarity on the type of service or product you are going to offer your ideal audience member.

You already came up with a quick answer to this in the first question in this section. It's now time to flesh that out as well. So, take that line once again from question one of this section and rewrite it here so it's on top of your mind as you complete this exercise.

What I can offer: _____

To whom: _____

How they will benefit: _____

CLARIFY YOUR VALUE

Given your ideal audience avatar, see if you can expand your offer further by answering the following questions: where you will make the offer, when, how and at what price. You can apply this thinking even if you're looking for employment. Think about where you want to work, what pay scale you want to negotiate, and the type of work you will want to do.

Let's get more specific on the value of your offer.

1. The service or product I will offer:

2. How I will make this offer available:

3. Where I will make it available:

4. When and how often it will be available:

5. How much I'll price it at/what will I negotiate for:

6. How I will package my product or service:

7. How will I promote my product, service or myself:

8. Additional bonuses or services I can add to sweeten my offer:

9. Other insights:

> *"Change your life today. Don't gamble on the future, act now, without delay."*
> — Simone de Beauvoir

MY SERVICE QUESTION 4

That was some great brainstorming to start the ball rolling. Bravo.

For the final exercise in this section (and we're almost done with this workbook), you'll need to put this book aside and spend some time researching. In the next pages, you will find nineteen specific ways to find the intersection between the work that brings you joy and the value you offer the world.

I didn't share this list earlier because I wanted to make sure you went through the thought process first and honed in on your interests. Bringing this list in at the start could have led to analysis paralysis. But now that you have a better idea of the value you offer, to whom and under what circumstances, you can do further research to refine your answers.

This list isn't exhaustive. The ideas and resources can apply to many sectors, so I'd recommend finding more specific activities and sites that are most relevant to your field of interest and pursuing only those.

You don't have to try every one of these ideas. Most people jump in with both feet without doing any homework, praying their idea will work out, but have to backtrack half-way through. If you attempt even two suggestions from this list, you'll be a huge step ahead of the majority.

AVOID PARALYSIS

This research shouldn't take you months at this point. After you've taken action, got the experience and talked to more people, you can return to this list and see what other areas you need to explore to refine your path further.

Planning and researching are iterative processes, which means you research and learn, and then you test and take action. Then, you rinse and repeat.

When you do research, especially at the beginning of a journey, you can go down meandering rabbit holes and get distracted by all sorts of shiny objects. It's important to make a plan and stay focused—which we'll do in the next page.

Make sure to give yourself a time limit of not more than four weeks for this part. Focus on the most relevant activities, then come back and finish the final section of this book. You'll progress faster and will feel more satisfied with yourself if you do.

For some of you this research may feel like overkill. And you may want to skip this part.

It's up to you, but I wouldn't recommend it. Setting aside four weeks to figure out what value you can give to others, so you can narrow your future work prospects and get paid for your passions will be well worth it.

EVERY NO IS ONE STEP CLOSER TO A YES

A large part of this research includes reaching out to people.

While some people you meet may not be able to help you right away, they may be able to in the future, so make a good impression and keep in touch. Following up with those you meet is gold.

It's best to enter any relationship asking yourself what you can do for them as much as what they can do for you. But never try to sell on the first encounter or even the second for that matter (it's a huge turnoff), and always keep the promises you make.

And think of every "no" as a step closer to a "yes." Those who succeed are those who try, test, fine-tune and keep going just like the good old Energizer Bunny.

Here are some successful people who didn't let anything stop their dreams. They were rebuffed many times, yet they persisted. They were determined to find the intersection between their talents, their joy, and their value to others, no matter what. If they can do it, so can we.

- Agatha Christie got rejected five years in a row before she ultimately got a publishing deal. Her book sales total in the billions now.
- Oprah was considered unsuitable for television because she showed too much emotion. Look where that got her.
- J.K. Rowling was a single mother living on minimum wage, with a dream to one day become a full-time author. Her publisher warned her to keep her day job.
- Lady Gaga was dropped only six months after signing to her first major record label. You can bet they're regretting that decision.
- Lucille Ball, one of the most iconic American actors, was recommended by her own drama instructors to try another profession.

If you did the previous exercises in this workbook with intention, the ideas you have percolating in your head will be those you have a passion for. When you are keen about something, you will persevere through any rejection. Remember, failure is temporary and only an opportunity to learn.

DO THE THINGS YOU'VE NEVER DONE BEFORE

Getting the things you've never had before means doing the things you've never done before. So, be brave and step out with confidence.

Yes, this will take time and effort, and in a few cases, it might cost you a few dollars. But this is an investment in your future.

"I love to see a young girl go out and grab the world by the lapels. Life's a bitch. You've got to go out and kick ass."
Maya Angelou

RESEARCH IDEAS

This list is in ascending order according to the time and effort it takes to do each activity.

Pick up the accompanying worksheet booklet for *Your Rebel Dreams* to get the website links related to the idhttps://www.RebelDivas.com/rebel-dreams-gifts/eas discussed below. Visit this website to get your private copy:

https://www.RebelDivas.com/rebel-dreams-gifts/

This booklet is shared separately, as these site addresses may need to be updated more frequently than this book.

1. Set up your profile on relevant online channels and social media forums so your thousand true fans can find you. Share your ideas on these platforms via posts and questions, and spur others to get in contact with you or engage in a discussion about your idea. Remember, you'll be more successful if you share and interact before pitching or asking for something.

2. If your plan is to start a small business or sell a service, do an online survey to find out what others might be looking for in your area of interest.

3. There are courses and podcasts on just about every topic in the world now. Head on over to some of the largest online course platforms, choose the area you're interested in and register for a class.

4. Skim online job boards to find what kind of work there is in your field of interest. Don't limit yourself to job descriptions, but they can be useful to better understand the needs and openings out there.

5. If you want to get into the online business world, experiment with online ads or promotions offered by Amazon, Facebook, Google, and others and use them (wisely) to understand what your target market is looking for.

6. Do informational interviews. Pick up the phone and call organizations or groups who would want your talents as an employee or a service provider. Find people who work in your field, reach out to them, and ask questions. Take them out for coffee or breakfast if they're in town. Read their books and articles before you meet them. Just like in real-life relationships, it's best to say hello and get to know them before springing an invitation or making a request.

7. Join local business or community groups or chambers of commerce where your potential customers or partners meet and introduce yourself. Make new connections and ask questions about your idea. Never worry about anyone stealing your idea. Implementation of an idea—which is what you plan to do, right?—is always far more valuable than the idea itself. Ideas are a dime a dozen.

8. Create a meetup and hold a seminar or talk on the topic you want to embark on to gauge interest in your idea. This may help you establish credentials before even starting out. This will also give you a captive audience to ask questions and probe your idea further. Don't

forget to look for existing meetups in your field and visit them to network, learn the industry or meet prospective partners or potential employers.

9. Attend a local community college course or a professional development seminar or conference on your topic and network with like-minded folk. Your instructors will be valuable resources to tap into. Business schools host seminars as a side hustle these days and can offer opportunities for you to access key people in industries easily.

10. Create a small pilot version of your product, service, art, music, or app (with basic functionality to start) and share it with a few people whom you think would be interested. It's important not to reach out to family and friends here, but to seek out strangers who'll give you honest feedback. Use their feedback to make adjustments and improvements to your pilot project.

11. Test your idea, especially if it's something you can offer online, on a freelance platform to gauge interest from a larger market. If your offer is taken up and you get good reviews, make sure to increase your price accordingly.

12. Create a short e-book that can be digested in thirty minutes or so and give it away as a lead magnet. Make sure to ask for email addresses or names in return for anyone getting your book so you can build an audience. Ask them for feedback, and in return promise them a follow-up mini e-book or a quiz or a related article as a gift. This is a great way to create a committed fan base who will root for you and give you tips along the way.

13. Take your product or service, especially if it's artisanal, to local farmers' markets or fairs. Rent a table and see how well it does, and watch carefully how people interact with the product and with you and listen to what they say. Use their feedback to adjust and improve your idea.

14. Talk to local businesses or restaurants and ask if they'd be willing to showcase your work, whether it's to put up your artwork or host your garage band. This is a great way to test your ideas because your neighbors will normally be more forgiving of newbies, and the audience is small enough that you don't have to worry too much about making mistakes.

15. Look for organizations or groups in the field you're interested in and ask to volunteer in exchange for an opportunity to learn or gain access to people in the industry. This may take time to do and you will need to build rapport, but it's well worth a try. This is one way to build long-term connections with people who could become your champions and mentors.

16. If you are already an expert to some degree in your field, create an online course and test a few modules on one of the online course platforms. Make it a pilot so you don't have to polish it, but use it to gauge interest and get feedback. If your students like what you provided, you can expand the course, for a fee of course.

17. Create videos and put them online and drive traffic to them via social media posts on other platforms. Making videos can be intimidating for some of us (it is for me) but with a bit of practice, anyone with a mobile phone can post fairly decent and attractive content in a matter of minutes. Test it out.

18. If you are thinking of a larger business idea which may require funds you don't have, you can join local business incubators where they provide training and information and also teach how to seek venture capital and from whom. They normally teach how to put business plans and pitches together, give you opportunities to practice, and also help make connections for you. Some of these incubators keep their costs low to attract small start-ups and may even be funded by the government.

19. Depending on where you live, you may have access to resources, funds and education opportunities provided by your local municipality or government. You can always find free classes on job search skills for students or new moms or others entering the job market. I've seen low-cost and even free courses targeted at new entrepreneurs and start-ups. Take advantage of these services, as they were designed to help people just like you.

Your Rebel Dreams

> *"I don't focus on what I'm up against.
> I focus on my goals and I try to ignore
> the rest."*
> Venus Williams

RESEARCH PLAN

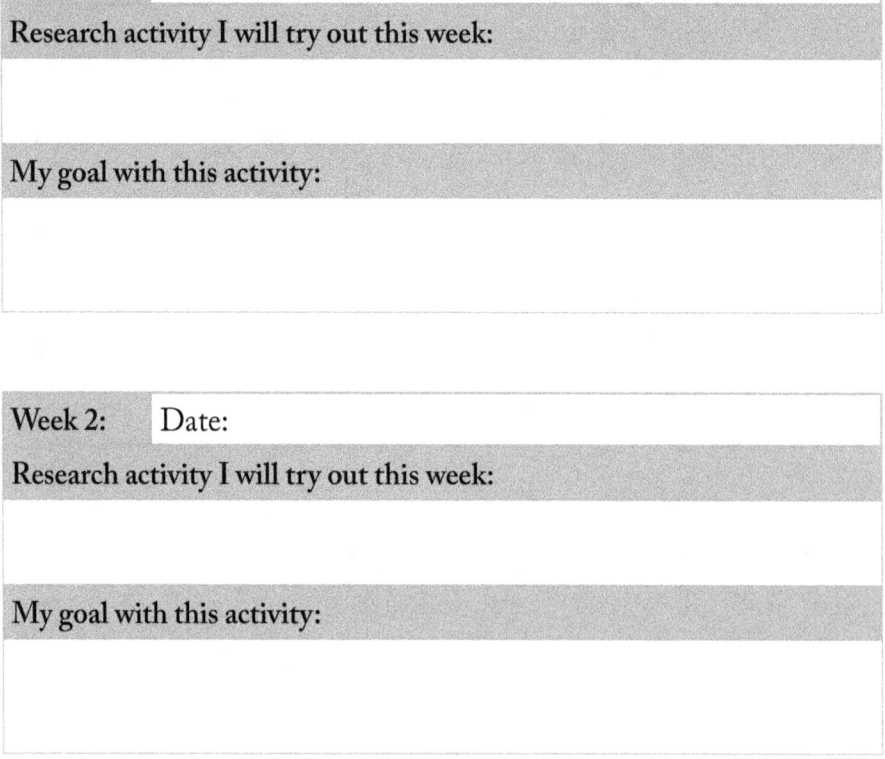

Here's a plan to help you focus.

Week 1:	Date:
Research activity I will try out this week:	
My goal with this activity:	

Week 2:	Date:
Research activity I will try out this week:	
My goal with this activity:	

Week 3: Date:

Research activity I will try out this week:

My goal with this activity:

Week 4: Date:

Research activity I will try out this week:

My goal with this activity:

Answer the question below before you go any further.

My deadline to finish this preliminary research and come back to the workbook is:

Date:

SO, HOW DO YOU FEEL?

That's the end of this section. Write down anything that wasn't captured in the questions but that you want to get out of your system or share on paper.

1. How do you feel after completing this section?

- ○ Meh. Nothing interesting here
- ○ I really want to get this, but I'm lost and need help
- ○ I'm doing well. Just need to think some more
- ○ Fantastic. I've nailed this round. Woo-hoo!
- ○ Other: _____

2. Where do you still need to figure things out more?

A.

B.

C.

3. What actions will you take in the next seven days to keep this topic on the top of your mind and clarify it further?

A.

B.

C.

RESEARCH BREAK

Take the next four weeks to follow the plan you made in this section. Read up on your field of interest. Talk to as many people as you can. Test your idea and ask yourself and others questions.

The next section is the most exciting part of this book because it's where you'll bring everything together! When you're ready and have completed all the previous sections come on back over, and turn the page.

See you in four weeks.

Your Rebel Dreams

WEEK NINE

Let's explore our possibilities.

SECTION SIX MY VISION

This section culminates with your vision and a vision boarding exercise.

I choose to make the rest of my life the best of my life.

Louise Hay

"Champions are made, not born."
Unknown

LIFE IS A GIFT

Do you know what the chances of you being born were? It's one in four hundred trillion.

That's one in 400,000,000,000,000!

How mind-boggling is that?

We've all been given one shot at this thing called life, a life that had crazy odds to begin with. Every day we have on this earth is a gift.

And for some of us, we have the privilege of living in a part of the world that has all the modern necessities, amenities, and conveniences on the planet. Not everyone has the same opportunities we have, so how can we then, in our right mind, squander this precious gift called life?

OUR POTENTIAL

Take a look around you.

Everything you see, every building, road, bridge, vehicle, every piece of furniture, room fixture, technological gadget, the art hanging on your wall or the books in your bookcase, were all created by people. Yes, human beings.

People like you and me took the steps to make these things happen. These things, however spectacular they may be, didn't appear magically. They weren't created by aliens or fairies, but by people who live or have lived on this Earth with us.

What makes you think you can't do the same? What makes you think you're different?

Aren't you a person too, a magnificent human with a brain that can imagine, think, plan, and create? And with a heart that can hope, wish, dream, and believe?

So what's holding you back? Is it a misconception of your past, your background, your gender, your race or your financial status?

Many people who have done great things started in dire adversity, probably in worse circumstances than you are in today.

But they didn't let that trip them up or stop them from achieving their dreams. It's surprising how many uber-successful people have overcome hardship—at times unimaginable difficulties—before they got to the top.

Just look at Oprah Winfrey, who was a rape victim at nine years old and pregnant by thirteen. She grew up in an era when segregation was still the law in her state. Look at Tony Robbins, who was neglected and abused as a child. Look at Jim Carrey, who lived in a van with nothing else to his name before becoming successful. Look at Charlize Theron, who witnessed her mother kill her father as a child. And look at Richard Branson, who was a poorly performing student with dyslexia.

Did you know that sixty-two percent of billionaires (yes, that's with a "b") in the USA are self-made? What does this tell you?

Granted America is a nirvana for entrepreneurs and has fewer societal restrictions for anyone with a good idea, gumption and grit. I know from personal observation this is not the case in many other parts around the world where misogyny, nepotism and corruption are still rampant. Maybe you live in one of those countries and feel a little disheartened. Still, doesn't this give you a taste of hope?

These billionaires are no different than you and me.

They have the same senses and brainpower as we do. They have the same juices inside them as us. They even have the same courage you and I have access to.

All they've done is controlled the primitive part of their brain, taken a deep breath in, and focused on their craft with the conviction that anything is possible. Their "overnight success" was usually several years in the making.

They put their hours in, taught themselves new skills, worked hard, made mistakes, got back up, learned quickly and improved every single day.

The only thing stopping you from moving forward and living the life you desire is *you*.

BREAK FREE

It's time to break free of those shackles that hold you back. It's time to push away those ugly fears and become the shiniest version of yourself.

Know that whatever you can imagine, you can be with enough courage, effort and time.

This is true whether you want to start a bakery or become a teacher, whether you want to be an aeronautics engineer and join NASA or kick off your very own business. Instead of sleepwalking through life and sacrificing yourself to a soul-crushing existence to build someone else's dream, you'll finally follow your own.

Yes, chasing your dreams can be hard work, but the funny thing is—and I say this from my own experience—when you find what you love to do, it no longer feels like work. I itch to get started in the morning, seven days a week.

And that feeling of freedom is worth everything.

BE A REBEL

If you want to become part of the top percentile that achieves their dreams, you've got to become a rebel.

So, while your colleagues lounge around the water cooler complaining about bad bosses or nasty commutes, you'll be busy designing the life you dream about. While your family members lie on the couch in front of the television every night, you'll be working on your goals.

It will take effort to get out of your comfort zone and take those first few steps, but it'll be worth it. No matter what anyone says, go ahead and do it anyway.

There is only one you on this planet. How can you not make your life the best it can be? How can you not make this a worthwhile voyage full of passion?

If you think about it, it's almost irresponsible of us not to pursue our dreams.

"*Life is short. If there was ever a moment to follow your passion and do what matters most to you, it is now.*"
Unknown

BRINGING IT ALL TOGETHER

Let's bring everything you've done in this workbook together. I promise you this final section will be the most exciting part of this journey.

So far, you've identified five significant aspects of your life: your values, your flair, the environment you desire to immerse yourself in, the work that brings you joy and the service you can offer others. This is quite an accomplishment. Most people go to their graves without unearthing even one-tenth of what you've learned.

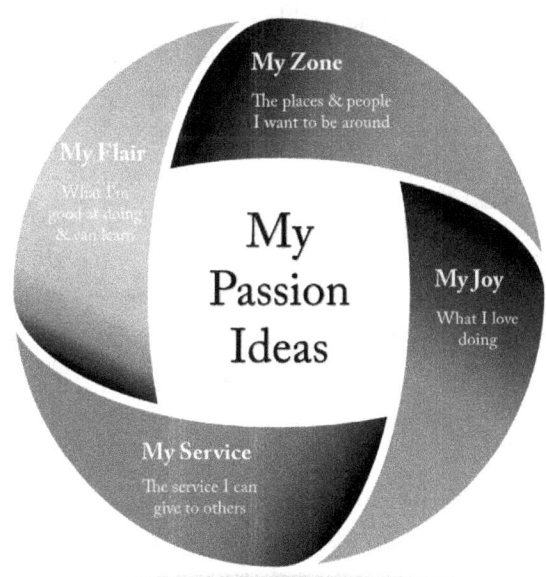

My Circle of Values

It's important to remember that none of these areas exist in a vacuum. We must look at this picture holistically to identify our passions in life—passions that will meet all our unique needs to create a dream life that is sustainable in the long run.

Everything you do needs to fall within your circle of fundamental values. Otherwise, it's a surefire path to creating a conflicted and miserable life. Then, within this circle of values, you will need to find the sweet spot where your joy, your flair, your zone and your service come together.

This is what we're going to explore in this section.

IMPORTANCE OF CONVERGENCE

Let's go through our options, one by one.

Convergence of Joy and Flair:
If you find work you love doing and have the talent for it or can improve by learning, you may feel like you've hit the jackpot. But if your environment is toxic, you may not get far. You'll find yourself spending more time fending off that negativity rather than honing your craft and enjoying your work in peace.

Convergence of Joy and Zone:
If you find work you love doing in an environment you enjoy being in, but you don't have the right skills or the opportunity to learn, you won't be happy for long. This might satisfy you in the short-term but very soon, you'll start to feel frustrated.

Convergence of Flair and Zone:
If you find work you're good at in an environment you love being in, but you find no joy in the work you do, that will surely make you feel dejected.

This is where most people find themselves today—working hard at jobs and many even getting good at it, but lacking joy in their days.

Convergence of Joy, Flair, and Zone:
Imagine a life where you'll be doing the work you love, work you've got talent for or can learn, in an environment where you thrive with people who care for you. How amazing would that be, right? But you'll only be able to sustain this if what you do provides a value for others. Even if you're fortunate to have a patron or someone who supports you, this won't be a fulfilling way to live.

Convergence of Joy, Flair, Zone and Service:
Now, what if you find the spot where all four touchstones meet?

Imagine finding work you enjoy that uses your innate talents in an environment you love being in, while at the same time bringing value to others—value others can benefit from and pay you for. How awesome would that be?

This is what will create a meaningful life where the work you do will sustain both your soul and your wallet in the long-term.

This is the sweet spot where you must look for your passion ideas.

❋❋❋

MY PASSIONS

My Passions = My Flair + My Zone + My Joy + My Service

Remember this equation from the beginning?

Your sweet spot is where your passions meet all your unique personal needs. If you can make your way into this place, you'll open yourself to fantastic possibilities.

Your Rebel Dreams

You'll find a higher level of success and satisfaction. You'll find yourself jumping out of bed looking forward to every single day. You'll become the person who says, "I feel awesome!" whenever someone asks how you're doing.

Wouldn't we all want to be in this sweet spot?

*"I'm tough, ambitious, and I know exactly
what I want. If that makes me a bitch, okay."*
Madonna

MY SWEET SPOT

Let's figure out how you can find what this sweet spot holds for you.

Given the incredible work you've done so far, you should now be able to fill with confidence the four circle diagram below using the final answers you gave for your flair, your zone, your joy and your service sections.

Refer back to your answers in these sections to make sure you don't miss anything or stray off path. But if you truly contemplated each exercise and gave thoughtful answers, the ideas are bubbling inside you and are eagerly waiting to be put down here. The work you did up front is now going pay off in spades.

Don't worry if you haven't come up with "perfect" answers or if you feel like you need to do more research. What you've done so far is impressive and is more than what ninety-nine percent of people do. After all that hard work, you can't go wrong with what you have.

Remember, perfection is a dream killer. You can always do more research later on and solidify your answers. It's imperative that you finish this section, so you can start taking action. This way, you'll also have something to refine should you need to.

As Martin Luther King Jr. said, "Faith is taking the first step even when you don't see the whole staircase." Have faith in yourself and in your passions. Take the first step, and the stairway to your life vision will unravel.

So start anyway. And start now.

Your Rebel Dreams

WHAT'S NEXT?

This exercise is a three-step jigsaw puzzle.

Step 1: In each circle below, jot down your main answers from the respective sections in the book: My Flair, My Zone, My Joy, and My Service.

Step 2: Sit back and look at how these four areas intersect. See if you can identify clues to where they come together seamlessly.

Step 3: Write down your thoughts that fit in where all four areas converge. You may have one or several ideas to note down here. These will be your passion ideas.

As you start filling these circles in, you might see areas that match well and others that don't. You might identify conflicts between some of these topics. It's best to see these mismatches now, rather than realize an important aspect of your plan won't work after you've spent time or even money.

Now is the time to play with your ideas with abundance.

You might find you have several passions, and that's perfectly fine. We'll prioritize them in the next exercise. For now, just let your imagination soar and put your ideas down. Have fun with this.

What's in your sweet spot?

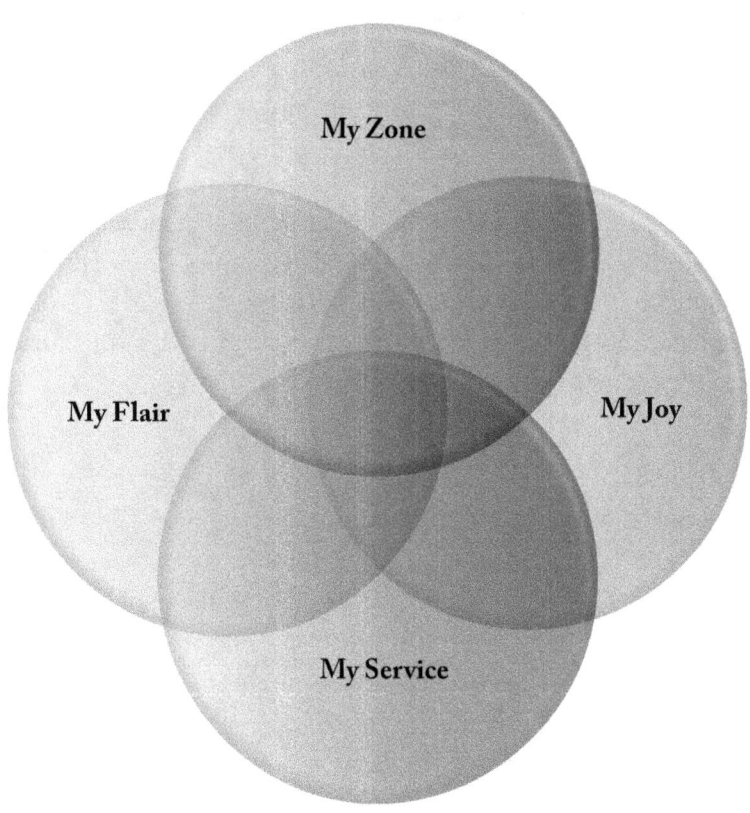

> *"Don't be intimidated by what you don't know. That can be your greatest strength and ensure that you do things differently from everyone else."*
> — Sara Blakely

YOUR PASSION IDEAS

Write down the top five passion ideas that lie in your sweet spot. Next to each one, see if you can write down the related values you identified in the first section, My Values.

If you have only one passion idea, that's great. That says you already have one good idea of what you want to pursue.

1. Passion idea
Related personal values:

2. Passion idea
Related personal values:

3. Passion idea

Related personal values:

4. Passion idea

Related personal values:

5. Passion idea

Related personal values:

LET'S PRIORITIZE

This list is a great start, but most of us can't do everything we want at the same time. It's important to stick with one passion idea and take it unwaveringly all the way to the end. Once you do that, there's nothing stopping you from realizing a new dream, right? The point is to focus on **One Thing**. Otherwise, you'll get pulled in all directions, find yourself distracted and not get anything achieved.

So what should you pay attention to first? How can you prioritize this list to find your One Thing?

Look over your list and pick the one passion idea that has the greatest alignment with your personal values. This should be the one idea that you feel is right deep in your bones.

Did you find the one idea that resonated with you the most? Write it down below.

My One Thing

Now, explore that.

"You can't fake passion."
Barbara Corcoran

EVERYTHING IS "FIGUROUTABLE."

Don't feel intimidated if this new passion idea is one you've never contemplated before. And don't think this is your be-all-and-end-all destination. There are many people who've made U-turns in their lives and have come out supremely successful. If something doesn't work out, you can always change course and try something else.

The best way to reduce the anxiety of starting anything new is to think of one single thing you need to do. This way, you're not looking at an enormous mountain you need to climb, just the next small step you can take. Start with the smallest action today. Then, the next. And the next.

Marie Forleo, superstar motivational speaker, educator, coach, and host of *Marie TV*, has a beautiful saying emblazoned on her studio wall: "Everything is figuroutable."

No matter what gets thrown our way, embracing an attitude that we can figure it out, that we always have options, is one of the most successful mindset shifts to instill in ourselves. Our human brains are more ingenious that we know. They can help us if only we let them.

Since you've chosen a passion that's near and dear to your heart, you'll find your way to the top, have no doubt about that.

Have faith in yourself and you will prevail. And you'll figure things out as you climb up. On the other hand, if you don't start at all, you'll be certain to never make your dreams come true.

MULTI-PASSIONATES

Humankind has never had such long life spans as we do today, and we've never been better equipped to remain healthy and fit for longer. This means we can try many things in our lifetime.

Here are some role models who followed multiple passions throughout their lives.

Julia Child was a top-secret government researcher before starting her cooking show at age fifty-one. Martha Stewart worked at Wall Street before heading her mega global business. Former American Army corps member Dorothy Davenhill Hirsch traveled to the North Pole when she was eighty-nine years old, well after retirement. Australian equestrian Mary Hanna became her country's oldest Olympian at sixty-one and believes she's just hitting her prime.

Most of the biggest rising entrepreneurial stars today are women over fifty who had become successful in their professional careers and are now embracing a different dream. Age was never a limitation to these wonder women who followed all their passions.

Our greatest deception is how little we think we're capable of. We get in our own way. We have our entire remaining life to try all the new things we're yearning to do!

FOCUS

For now, your next step will be to focus on your One Thing.

Here's what you'll need to do: practice your craft, find the right mentors, talk to people, share your results, and see how it works. If you find, through this process, that the outcome is not what you're looking for, you can always come back and try out another passion idea from this list.

The great thing is you've already identified your fundamental values and needs. You know what your talents are, what environments you like to be in, what work brings you joy and what value you can give others. So whatever passion idea you choose, you can't go wrong.

> *"If your dreams don't scare you,*
> *they're not big enough."*
> *Ellen Johnson Sirleaf*

NEXT STEP

Let's take your One Thing—the prominent passion idea you've chosen to focus on—and write it down as a vision statement. This will help you to come up with the right goals and action steps to turn your passion idea into reality.

Here are the questions you need to answer at this final stage:

1. What's your end goal for pursuing this passion idea?

2. What will your life look like as you work on this passion idea?

3. How will you feel when you've become successful at it?

MY BIG AUDACIOUS VISION

Using these answers, can you now translate your passion idea into a big audacious vision?

This statement should give you goose bumps on your arms, knowing you'll be pursuing this wonderful new path. Now is not the time to shrink or be timid. You didn't go through all this soul-searching to take just a small step outside your porch, did you? Don't even think of the sky as a limitation.

Dream big. Then dream even bigger, darling.

Now, write it down.

My Big Audacious Vision:

You don't need to figure out *how* you'll achieve your vision yet.

None of the great change-makers knew exactly how they were going do what they dreamed of doing. What they had, however, was a clear vision of their passions, and this is where we want to be.

We'll figure out the *how*, including how to set goals and make an action plan, when we get to the second Rebel Diva workbook, *Your Rebel Plans*.

> *"We never know how high we are till we are called to rise; And then, if we are true to plan, our statures touch the skies."*
> Emily Dickinson

YOUR JOURNEY HAS BEGUN

Some people take decades to find their passions. Others putter around dabbling in everything but never find their true path. Most people end up in their graves never even having tried to discover their passions. You, on the other hand, have begun your journey to a fulfilled life that is authentic to you.

You're standing in your own power as a Rebel Diva. Congratulations.

VISUALIZE YOUR FUTURE

Writing out your vision dramatically enhances the likelihood of success. Even more compelling is a visual representation of your future. Images capture your attention faster, and their pull is stronger than mere words on paper.

To increase the chances of your success, create a collage of images that reflect your vision. Yes, you're going to make a vision board.

START WITH THESE QUESTIONS

Take out some old magazines or go online (www.Pinterest.com is great) and start rooting for pictures that reflect your Big Audacious Vision. Pick the images that resonate with you the most. Showcase the lifestyle you see yourself enjoying as you work on your passion idea as well as after you achieve your vision.

If you need a few tips to start this vision board, ask yourself the following questions:

- What work will I be doing?
- Who will I be surrounded by?
- What will my family life be like?
- Where will I be living and with whom?
- What will be my ideal day?
- What will I be doing for fun and leisure?
- What will my environment look like—in all the areas I occupy?
- Who will be my mentors, colleagues, partners?
- What results will I have achieved?
- What accolades or recognition will I have received?
- Who will I have touched, and who will have touched me?
- Whose lives will I have improved with my big audacious goal?

Let your imagination soar and your creative juices take over.
It's vision boarding time. Have fun.

Your Rebel Dreams

Rebel Diva

VISION BOARD

Paste your images here or do this online or on a Pinterest board (www.Pinterest.com). Use the tool you'll enjoy the most.

Tikiri

> *"Create the highest, grandest vision possible for your life, because you become what you believe"*
> Oprah Winfrey

LIVE YOUR VISION

I look at my vision board every day to remind myself of the future I'm creating for myself. This motivates me to make sure everything I do that day is in alignment with it.

Every morning, after a ten-minute meditation on my yoga mat when my mind is relaxed and open, I set a timer, place my one-page vision board in front of me, and go through it. This embeds the dream in my mind and gets me excited about the work I do. This also helps me to take failures in stride because I know my journey is still unraveling, and my vision is bigger than one mistake. It keeps my spirits up, my motivation high, and my work on track.

This simple exercise can also dissipate any remaining doubt you may have in yourself or in your big vision. You'll start to stand a little straighter and feel a little stronger. You'll find your confidence expand, and most importantly, it will spur you to take action right away to realize your vision.

VISION EVERY DAY

Here's a simple five-step process to help you entrench your vision in your psyche and accelerate your dreams:

1. Schedule ten minutes every day, preferably first thing in the morning. Find a trigger that will remind you it's visioning time. Mine is finishing my daily meditation practice.

2. Find a comfortable spot where you'll be undisturbed. Make this your sacred space and stick to it.

3. Every day at your scheduled time, go to this quiet place, sit comfortably with your vision board in front of you, and set a ten-minute timer.

4. Go through your vision board, image by image, talking out loud to yourself. Tell yourself what each image means to you. Visualize your future in your mind.

5. Be aware of the feelings that come as you look at each image. Let these emotions rise in you. Let them seep into every cell in your body and let them spread through your nervous system. Immerse yourself in those feelings. Do this for every single image on your vision board until the timer goes off.

THE POWER OF I AM

Our beliefs in ourselves are the most powerful indicators of success.

Our strongest drive as human beings is to remain consistent with how we define ourselves, that is, the words we normally use after saying "I am…"

One way to counteract negative sentiments that can trip you up in life is to create I am sentences from your vision board. As you look through each image every morning, make it even more compelling by saying "I am…" Stay away from sentences that start with "I will…," which is future oriented, or "I won't…," which opens the door to negative emotions.

When you say "I am…" often enough, you'll begin to believe it and gravitate toward taking action that makes you exactly that kind of person. This is the most effective way to embed your vision in your mind.

EXAMPLE

Let's take a situation many people grapple with. If you're constantly saying "I'm fat," whatever diets you follow will only work in the short-term, if at all. This is why New Year's resolutions don't stick, because they're nothing more than fleeting wish lists. If you really want to make a change, you have to *believe* in that new version of you first.

If you think, believe, and tell yourself daily "I'm a healthy person," you'll inevitably take the necessary actions to becoming and staying healthy. You'll opt for healthy choices and stay away from sugary products or fried foods. You'll take the stairs up instead of the elevator. In short, you'll find yourself doing what you have to do to be the person you believe you are.

This is far more effective than setting annual resolutions. Rather than say, "I want to lose ten pounds by April," tell yourself, "I'm a healthy, fit, and beautiful woman." Say this with meaning and emotion every day, and watch how you'll invariably start doing the things that will make you fit and healthy—and by extension feel confident and look beautiful.

Let's use this technique for our vision board. Based on your vision, write down five main *I am* sentences, imagining you're already living your dream life. Say these out loud every day.

Who I Am:

1. I am:	
2. I am:	
3. I am:	
4. I am:	
5. I am:	

WEEK NINE CONTINUED

SECTION SEVEN MY PLEDGE

My promise to myself

Your Rebel Dreams

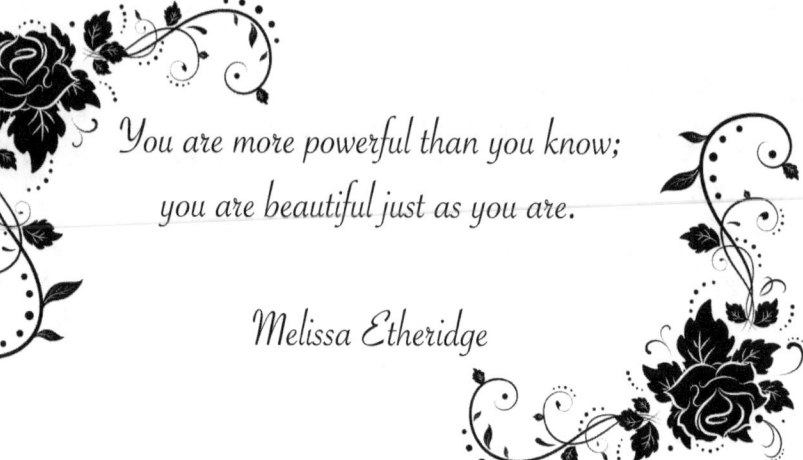

You are more powerful than you know; you are beautiful just as you are.

Melissa Etheridge

*"Success is getting what you want.
Happiness is wanting what you get."*
Ingrid Bergman

A RECAP

Let's do a check of how far you've come.

Go back to the first ever question you answered in the Introduction—*Where Am I Today?* Take a look at the statements you made, and then look at the Big Audacious Vision you just crafted for yourself.

> 1. What differences do you see in how you thought about yourself then and how you view yourself now?

> 2. What have you learned about yourself from going through all these exercises?

> 3. Do you feel hopeful for your future? Invigorated? Excited?

Your Rebel Dreams

MY PLEDGE

Today, I pledge to take control of my future and live a life of no regrets.

I pledge to stand in my own power and never let anyone take it away from me.

I pledge to take action toward my vision and make my dreams come true.

I pledge to choose to be happy and find joy in life.

Signature	

Date	

Your Rebel Dreams

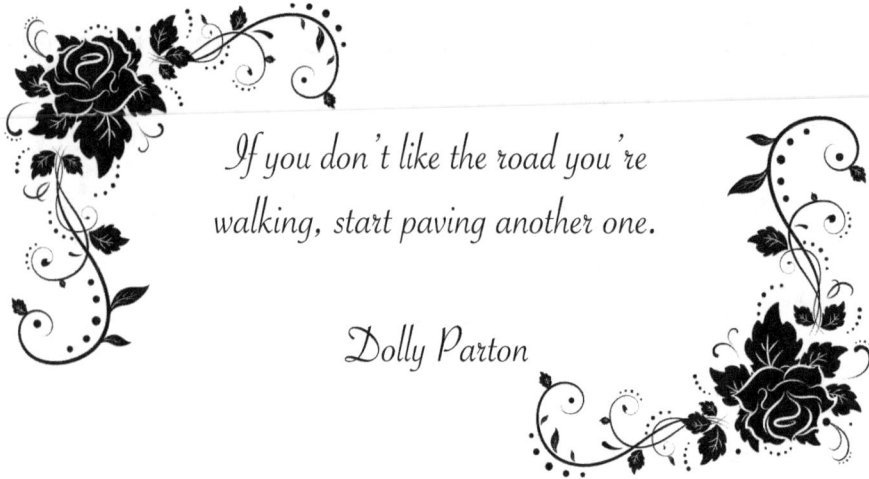

If you don't like the road you're walking, start paving another one.

— Dolly Parton

Tikiri

BONUS SECTION EIGHT

> "You can waste your lives drawing lines. Or you can live your life crossing them."
> Shonda Rhimes

BONUS QUESTION

Here is one last question for you. Create your very own bucket list here.

Before I die, I want to:
1.
2.
3.
4.
5.
6.
7.
8.
9.
10.

> "Stop wearing your wishbone where your backbone ought to be."
> Elizabeth Gilbert

FINAL WORD

There's much more to living your dream life than can be covered by the exercises here. This workbook's goal was to identify your purpose and your passions and come up with a vision for your life.

The second Rebel Diva book, *Your Rebel Plans*, will show you how to make that vision come alive. It will show you how to set smart goals, how to create an action plan and how to track your progress. This workbook is a practical, hands-on guide with easy-to-follow exercises that will show you how to achieve your Big Audacious Vision.

The third book, *Your Rebel Life*, shares the ten most important pillars of your life—from your physical and mental well-being to your finances and relationship health and more—and shows what you need to do in each area so you can live every day in happiness and health as you walk toward your life vision.

Good luck, and see you in the next book!

Your Rebel Dreams

"Just when the caterpillar thought the world was over, she became a butterfly."

English Proverb

Your Rebel Dreams

THANK YOU!

Thank you for dedicating time for yourself and for coming on this journey to create an amazing, shiny new you. Keep this book somewhere you can see every day to keep the momentum going. Go over your answers every month to check your progress and plan for the next year.

Get **YOUR REBEL PLANS**, the second Rebel Diva book, to continue your journey toward your life dreams.

Get Your Rebel Plans here: www.books2read.com/YourRebelPlans

SIGN UP TO GET YOUR EXCLUSIVE GIFT!

This Rebel Diva booklet comes with three essential decision-making tools to help you overcome any anxieties when faced with life's challenges. Click on the cover or go to the link below to get your free copy and also learn about exclusive and free training at the Rebel Diva Academy.

THE FEAR BUSTER

https://www.RebelDivas.com/rebel-dreams-gifts/

Come on over and join other Rebel Divas in our private Facebook Group: Rebel Divas to share your thoughts and dreams, learn new tips and get inspired.

https://www.facebook.com/groups/RebelDivas

Your thoughts mean a lot to me, and I'd love to hear your feedback. It's also how I'll be able to give you what you're looking for in the future. If you'd like to leave an honest review of this book, please do so here:

https://books2read.com/YourRebelDreams

THE REBEL DIVA SERIES

www.RebelDivas.com

The Rebel Diva books are practical guides to living the life you dream about.

They bring together lessons from the best self-help and personal development resources available today and synthesize them into simple guided exercises that anyone can follow without drowning in detail. These books give you the what you need to do as well as the how to follow through with tasks and activities.

The tools here are simple, but their reach is deep. They're designed to make you contemplate your past, present, and future, and empower you to become a visionary for your own life. All the answers are in you. All these workbooks do is extract them one gentle question at a time and make you write them down, so you can take the first steps toward your future.

These books are not meant to sit and look pretty on a bookshelf but to be marked up, highlighted, and dog-eared with your scribbling all over the pages. Keep them on your bedside table with a pen, so you can reach them whenever you need a jolt of inspiration or want to track your progress.

All you need to do is find one hour every week to go through one chapter in any of these books. Take the time to discover your life's purpose and learn how to stand in your own power. This is how you'll find the freedom to create the life you desire.

BOOK 1 - YOUR REBEL DREAMS

This book will show you how to uncover the amazing gifts you have in life.

You'll find a series of practical exercises that will help you create a vision for your life that matches your personal values and your unique personality. In this book, you'll discover your ultimate passions and purpose in life.

Once completed, you can check back with *Your Rebel Dreams* once a year. Make it the thing you do every December 31st, just before you head out to the New Year's Eve party. The benefits of spending an hour taking stock of the past year and planning for the next one will be invaluable.

The main sections in this book are:

1. My Values
2. My Flair
3. My Zone
4. My Joy
5. My Service
6. My Vision

BOOK 2 – YOUR REBEL PLANS

This book will show you how to make your dreams come alive.

You will go through a series of easy-to-follow exercises derived from sophisticated planning models. Step-by-step, they will help you identify your core goals and create an action plan for your life. You'll learn how to track your progress along the way and celebrate your successes. At the end of this workbook, you'll have a treasure map to your life dreams—a map that will help you stay on your game, no matter what.

Once completed, you can check back with *Your Rebel Plans* every three months to see how you're progressing. And to find a good excuse to reward yourself! You'll only need to spend thirty minutes each time to make sure you're on track.

The main sections in this book are:

1. My Goals
2. My Plans
3. My Check-ins

4. My Schedule
5. My Year

BOOK 3 – YOUR REBEL LIFE

This book will show you how to live a harmonious, happy and healthy life every single day.

You'll get access to one hundred tips for the ten most important facets of your life. These are the pillars of your life you need to pay special attention to if you want to be happy and fulfilled. Using these tips, you'll learn how to design a holistic lifestyle that's in tune with the fundamental values you identified in *Your Rebel Dreams* and the ambitions you wrote down in *Your Rebel Plans*.

This is a standalone guide and can be read anytime. Take a thirty-minute coffee break at the end of every month to take stock of where you are and apply one more tip to enhance your life.

The main sections in this book are:

My Environment:
1. Feel Well - My Environment Health

My Health:
2. Sleep Well - My Rejuvenation Health
3. Move Well - My Physical Health
4. Eat Well - My Nutrition Health

My Vocation:
5. Learn Well - My Knowledge Health
6. Work Well - My Career Health
7. Invest Well - My Wealth Health

My Spirit:
    8. Think Well - My Mental Health

    9. Love Well - My Relationship Health

    10. Play Well - My Spirit Health

ABOUT THE AUTHOR

Tikiri holds a bachelor's degree in international business from North America and a master's degree in management from Europe. She has over fifteen years experience managing large-scale projects and corporate risk management programs, and has studied, worked and lived in several countries across four continents.

Tikiri is the award-winning author of several fiction and nonfiction books and through her writing, champions women's and girl's rights around the world.

OKAY, ENOUGH OF THE FORMAL STUFF

My expertise doesn't come from a post doctorate psychology degree. Neither do I profess to be a self-help guru of any sort. I'm still a work in progress and try to learn something new every day.

I started small. Very small. I began my career trying to sell Kirby vacuum cleaners door-to-door (nope, I didn't sell even one) and graduated to cleaning toilets (made a lot more than my vacuum-selling stint). I did this to pay for rent, ramen noodles and tuition.

Like everyone else, I've muddled my way through life. I've been a traveler and an immigrant. I've been poor and desperate. I've been bullied and afraid. I've been heartbroken and devastated. And I'm a foreigner everywhere I go. Through all this, I've also seized opportunities to learn as much as I can, push myself and figure out how people think, behave and grow.

The most important lesson I've learned is if you stand in your power no matter what's going around you or how others treat you, things work out. They always do.

I've used my personal experiences and what I've learned from others to write these books. The lessons in here are what helped me create the life I desired, so I wrote these books hoping they will help you too in some way. Even if one sentence spurs you forward, I will have done my job.

To say hello and connect, come on over to www.TikiriHerath.com

OTHER BOOKS BY THE AUTHOR

The Red-Heeled Rebels Novel Series

The Red-Heeled Rebels is a gripping, coming-of-age, global suspense thriller with iron-willed heroines who fight villains and traditions that keep them down. If you like exotic locales, complex twists, and globe-trotting female leads, you'll love this series.

What readers are saying:

> "A wonderful story! I didn't want to leave the characters."

> "A real page turner and international thriller. Reminds me of why I've always loved to read. Because I can visit worlds and places I wouldn't ordinarily get to see."

> "If you love adventure, strong female leads and cultural insights, this is the perfect book for you."

> "A heart stopping adventure. I just couldn't put the book down till I finished reading it."

> "This is soul writing that needs to be read."

To claim the prequel story to this series for free go to

www.RedHeeledRebels.com

Your Rebel Dreams

Tikiri

Your Rebel Dreams

www.ingramcontent.com/pod-product-compliance
Lightning Source LLC
Chambersburg PA
CBHW070052080526
44586CB00013B/1029